eMoviePoster.com

presents

WARNER BROS. MOVIE POSTERS AT AUCTION

volume 23 of the illustrated history of movies through posters

Every item pictured in this book will be auctioned by **eMoviePoster.com** on the Internet from 12/09/04-12/19/04 (all items will close on 12/19 throughout that day). IT IS IMPORTANT TO NOTE THAT THIS BOOK PICTURES LESS THAN 20% OF THE ITEMS THAT WILL BE AUCTIONED ON 12/19! Complete detailed descriptions of every item in this most unusual auction (both the 576 pictured in this volume and the over 2,000 that are not), including high quality digital images and detailed condition descriptions) can be found on our website **http://www.emovieposter.com**

IN THIS AUCTION THERE ARE:
NO Buyer's Premiums
$8 U.S. Shipping Charge
(no matter how many items you buy)
NO Sales Tax (except in Missouri)
See our website for full details!

In addition to the auction of the items in this volume, THERE WILL BE ANOTHER REMARKABLE AUCTION OF MOVIE POSTERS12/08/04-12/18/04! Along with the items in the Warner Bros. collection, eMoviePoster.com will auction an amazing collection of 424 movie posters and lobby cards from many of the finest movies ever made, covering all years and genres, but with particular focus on horror and science fiction! This auction runs from December 8th to December 18th (see our website for full details).

IMPORTANT NOTICE:This publication is neither endorsed by or affiliated with the Warner Bros. movie studio. It contains images of a collection of movie paper memorabilia, assembled by a single individual over a 35 year period, all of which are being publicly auctioned. Note the the image of James Dean on the cover is enlarged detail from Item #355, and that the Warner Bros. logo is enlarged detail from Item #225.

Edited and Published by Bruce Hershenson
P.O. Box 874, West Plains, MO 65775
Phone: **(417) 256-9616** Fax: **(417) 257-6948**
mail@emovieposter.com (e-mail)
http://**www.emovieposter.com** (website)

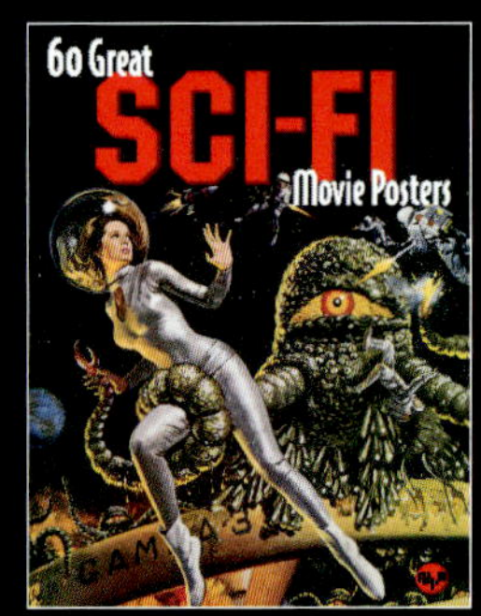

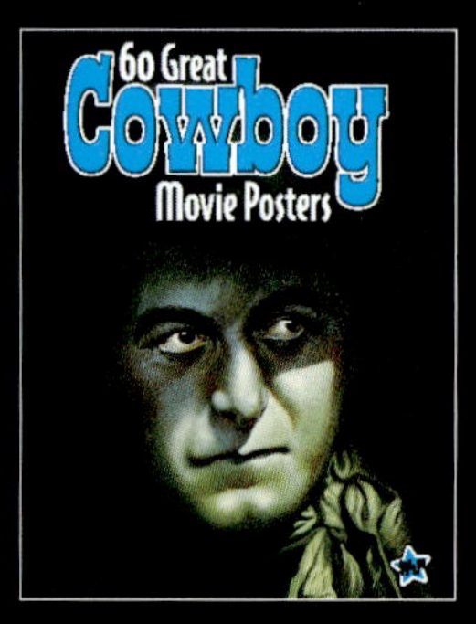

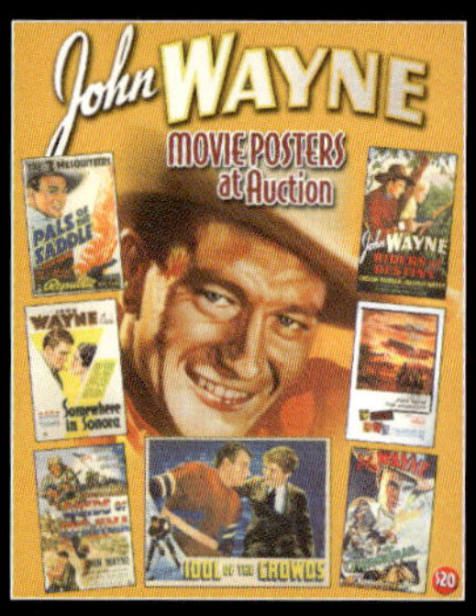

IF YOU ENJOYED THIS MOVIE POSTER BOOK, THEN YOU ARE SURE TO ENJOY THESE OTHER SIMILAR BRUCE HERSHENSON PUBLICATIONS. LOOK FOR THEM AT YOUR LOCAL BOOKSTORE OR ORDER THEM DIRECT FROM THE PUBLISHER.

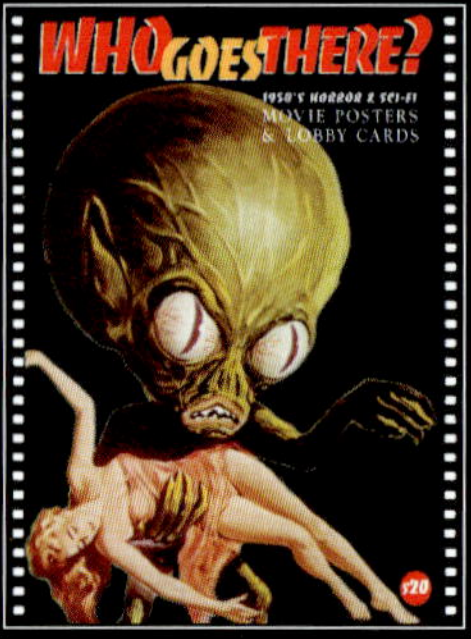

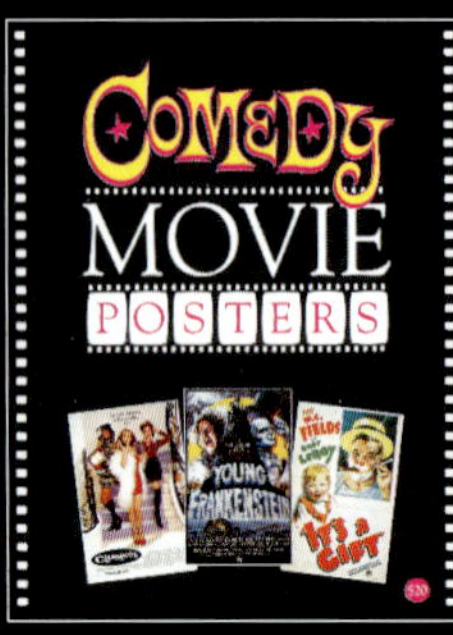

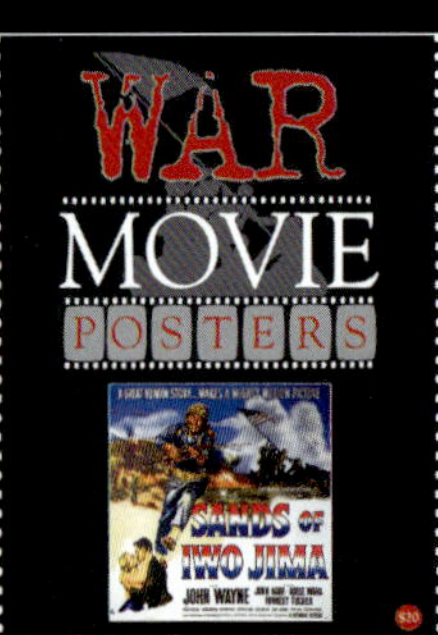

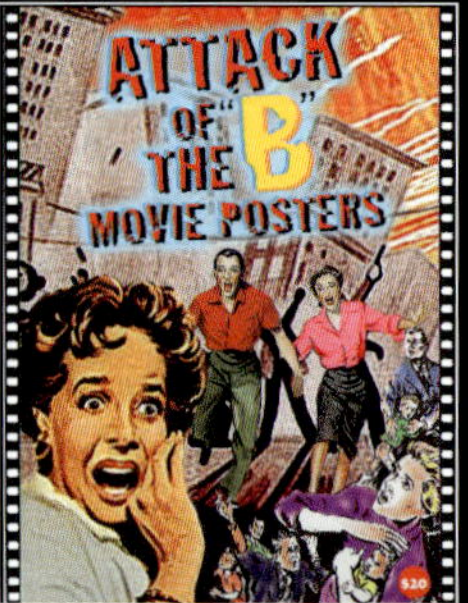

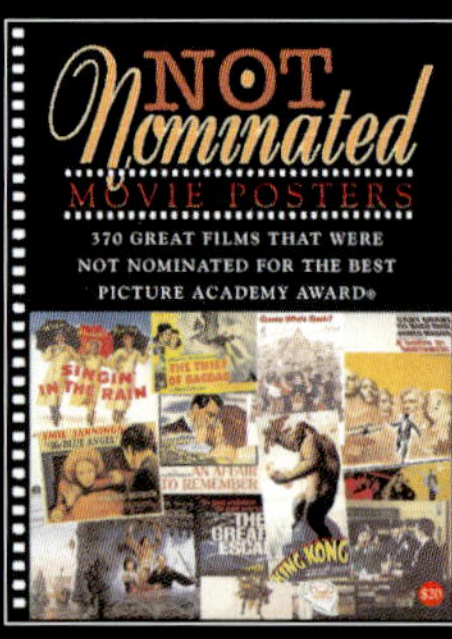

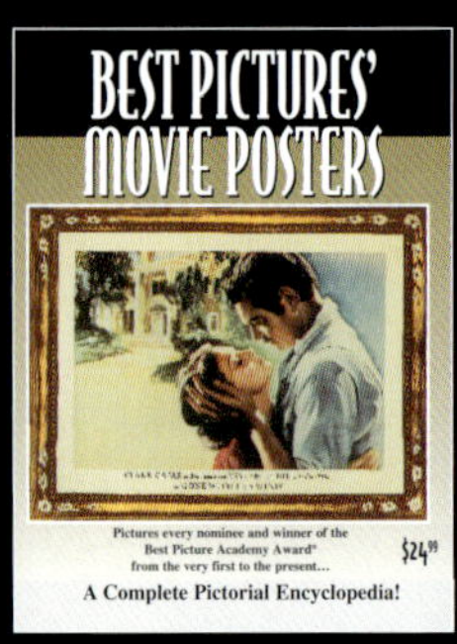

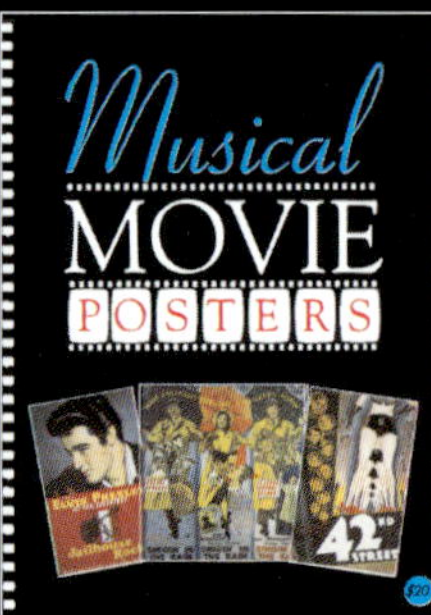

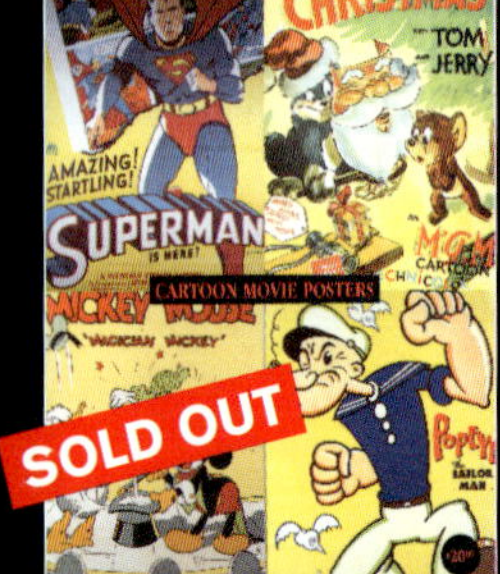

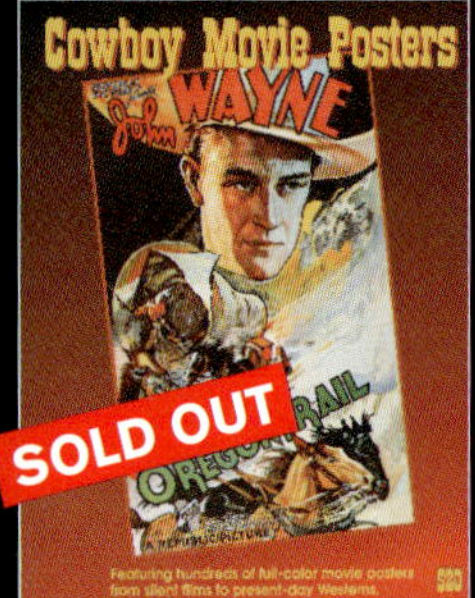

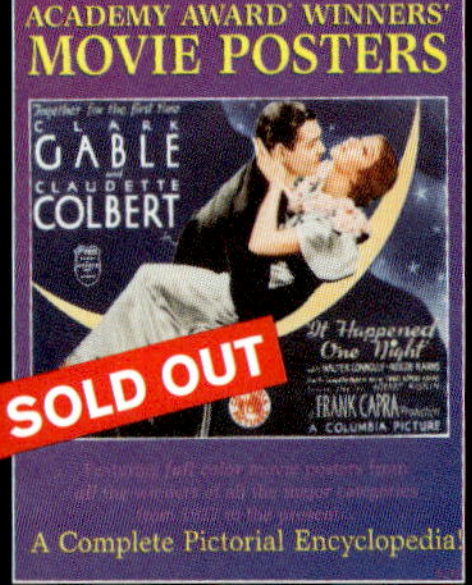

INTRODUCTION

My name is Bruce Hershenson and since 1990 I have sold over 23 MILLION dollars of vintage movie posters, much of it through public auctions. In 1990 I organized the very first all-movie poster auction ever held by a major auction house and since then I organized 12 more major "live" movie poster auctions (nine more for Christie's auction house and three for Howard Lowery auctions) with total sales of just under ten million dollars. In between, I sold over 30,000 movie posters and lobby cards through semi-annual sales catalogs with sales of over five million dollars.

In 2001 I decided to move my major auctions to the Internet. On June 30 and July 1, 2001 (in Vintage Hollywood Posters IV), I auctioned 711 items for a total of $717,000. Those who have purchased items at other major auctions are all too familiar with the many added fees tacked on after the auction's close, including a buyer's premium that ranges from 15% to 20%, and shipping fees that range from high to outrageous. But in THIS auction, Vintage Hollywood Posters IV, there were NO Buyer's Premium, NO U.S. Shipping charges, and NO Sales Tax (except in Missouri). This saved most buyers from 30% to 40%!

I also provided complete detailed descriptions of every item. Many major auctions only provide bidders with fuzzy images (sometimes "enhanced", and sometimes not of the exact item being purchased) and fuzzier condition descriptions, glossing over condition defects and restoration. I provided high quality unretouched digital images of the actual items being sold, and detailed condition descriptions (including detailed descriptions of each restored item's PRE-restoration condition, something NO other major auction house provides). In 2002-2004 I have repeated the process with Vintage Hollywood Posters V-VII, with sales of over half a million dollars per auction!

Most of my major auctions have been wide-ranging assortments of movie posters, covering all years and genres. Three times I have been consigned comprehensive collections focused on a single subject (once serial movie posters, once 1950s sci-fi movie posters, and once John Wayne posters). NOW I PRESENT MY FOURTH MAJOR AUCTION DEVOTED TO A SINGLE SUBJECT.

This auction is comprised of an amazing collection of over 2,500 movie posters, lobby cards and all sorts of other movie paper from a considerable percentage of all the movies the famed Warner Bros. studio ever made, from their humble beginnings in 1920 all the way through to the present day, with extra strong representation of their most major stars, such as Al Jolson, Rin Tin Tin, Errol Flynn, Bette Davis, James Cagney, Ronald Reagan, Humphrey Bogart, James Dean, Clint Easwood, etc, etc! This amazing collection was assembled over decades (and it is unlikely a similar collection could be amassed in a lesser amount of time, given the rarity of much of its contents!), but every item in it will be auctioned on December 19, 2004.

This auction, WARNER BROS. MOVIE POSTERS AT AUCTION, will end on 12/19/04 (there will be preliminary bidding from December 9-19). THERE ARE NO BUYER'S PREMIUMS, A REASONABLE $8 U.S. SHIPPING CHARGE (No matter how many items you buy), AND NO SALES TAX (except in Missouri), which will again save buyers 30% to 40%!

THERE WILL BE A REMARKABLE AUCTION OF MOVIE POSTERS AND LOBBY CARDS FROM 12/08/04-12/18/04!
Along with all the items in the Warner Bros. collection, eMoviePoster.com will auction an amazing collection of 424 movie posters and lobby cards from many of the finest movies ever made, covering all years and genres, but with particular focus on horror and science fiction! The auction runs from December 8th to December 18th (see our website for full details).

AN IMPORTANT ANNOUNCEMENT REGARDING THE POSTERS AND LOBBY CARDS IN THIS VOLUME!

All of the items pictured in this book are the first release one-sheet poster (if it is a vertical image) or a first release scene lobby card (if it is a horizontal image) unless otherwise noted under the image. All of the items will be auctioned by eMoviePoster.com on the Internet on 12/19/04. If you are reading this PRIOR to that date, go to http://www,emovieposter.com to find out how to bid (if you don't have Internet access, call 417-256-9616 and we,ll make arrangements for you to bid another way). If you are reading this AFTER 12/19/04, you will find a sheet added to this volume that gives the prices every item sold for. If you have items you would like us to consider for our future auctions, go to http://www.emovieposter.com/consign.htm and read our terms, or, if you don,t have Internet access, call us or mail us a list of your posters (see the first page of this book for full contact info). If you are interested in buying movie posters or lobby cards, or in learning more about the hobby, you should visit our website at http://www,emovieposter.com, where you will find thousands of images of the very best movie posters, as well as lots of information important to every collector.

You can find out all you need to know about bidding on items in this most exciting auction by going to my website, http://www.emovieposter.com where you can also view this entire catalog in an online digital format, INCLUDING THE OVER TWO THOUSAND ITEMS NOT PICTURED IN THIS CATALOG!

Phillip Wages (who created my online auctions and also much of my website) and Amy Knight (who did the layouts and cover design for this books and many of my previous books) gave considerable assistance in the preparation of this auction and this book, and I thank them very much. I dedicate this book to the latest addition to my family, Lucy Evalyn Hershenson!

Bruce Hershenson
December 2004

1. THE TIGER BAND, 1920, title card

2. MIRACLES OF THE JUNGLE, 1921, title card

3. MIRACLES OF THE JUNGLE, 1921

4. MIRACLES OF THE JUNGLE, 1921

5. THE BEAUTIFUL & THE DAMNED, 1922, title card

6. LITTLE JOHNNY JONES, 1923, title card

7. MAIN STREET, 1923, title card

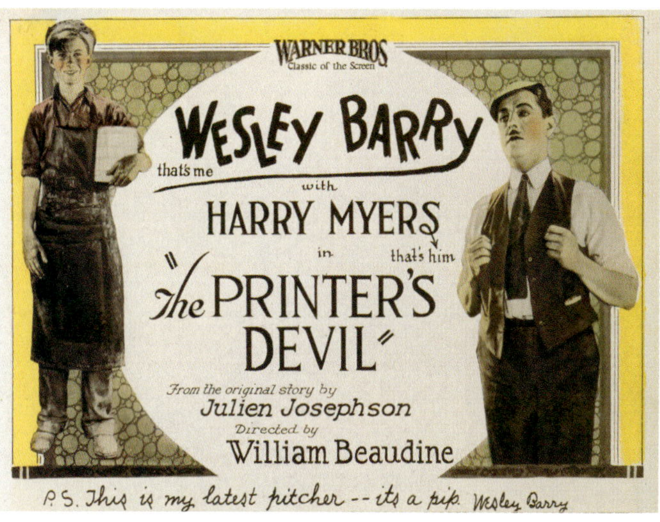

8. THE PRINTER'S DEVIL, 1923, title card

9. THE LOVER OF CAMILLE, 1924

10. BEAU BRUMMEL, 1924

11. LOVERS LANE, 1924, title card

12. THE MARRIAGE CIRCLE, 1924

13. BOBBED HAIR, 1925, title card

14. TRACKED IN THE SNOW COUNTRY, 1925, title card

15. HOW BAXTER BUTTED IN, 1925

16. THE TENTH WOMAN, 1925, title card

17. HOW BAXTER BUTTED IN, 1925

18. THE SEA BEAST, 1926, title card

19. THE GOLDEN COCOON, 1926, title card

20. GINSBERG THE GREAT, 1927

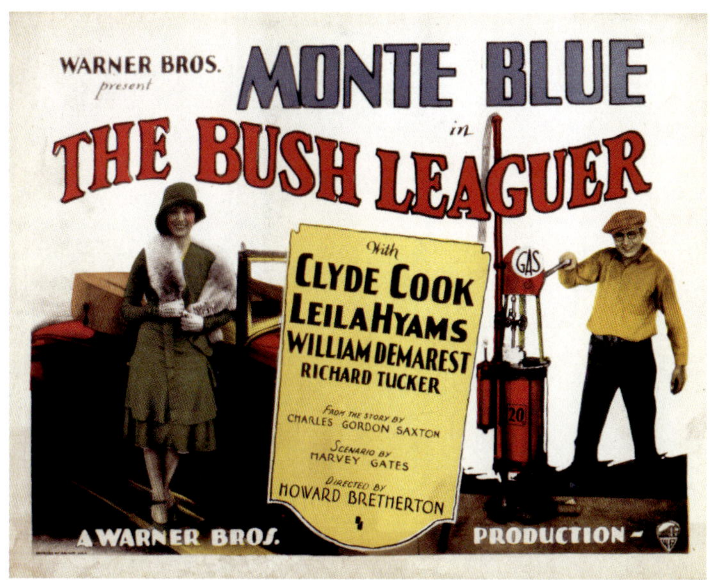

21. THE BUSH LEAGUER, 1927, title card

22. THE COLLEGE WIDOW, 1927

23. THE JAZZ SINGER, 1927

24. THE JAZZ SINGER, 1927

25. GOOD TIME CHARLEY, 1927, title card

26. HUSBANDS FOR RENT, 1927

27. IF I WERE SINGLE, 1927, title card

28. OLD SAN FRANCISCO, 1927, title card

29. SLIGHTLY USED, 1927, title card

30. WHAT HAPPENED TO FATHER, 1927, title card

31. THE SINGING FOOL, 1928

32. LIGHTS OF NEW YORK, 1928, title card

33. LILAC TIME, 1928, title card

34. RINTY OF THE DESERT, 1928, title card

35. STATE STREET SADIE, 1928, title card

36. THE BARKER, 1928

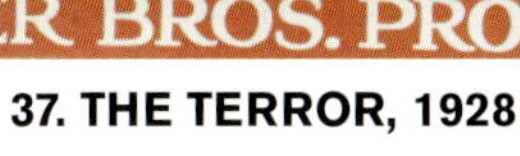

37. THE TERROR, 1928

38. SAY IT WITH SONGS, 1929

39. ON WITH THE SHOW, 1929

40. SONNY BOY, 1929

41. MAMMY, 1930, insert

42. THE GIRL OF THE GOLDEN WEST, 1930, Swedish

43. COURAGE, 1930

44. THE GIRLFRIENDS, 1930

45. THE DOORWAY TO HELL, 1930

46. GENERAL CRACK, 1930

47. TOP SPEED, 1930, title card

48. GOLD DUST GERTIE, 1931, title card

49. THE NAUGHTY FLIRT, 1931

50. THE STAR WITNESS, 1931

51. SVENGALI, 1931

52. BELIEVE IT OR NOT, 1931

53. ONE DAY STAND!, 1930

54. BROADWAY BREVITIES, 1935

55. JUST A CUTE KID, 1940/41

56. BROADWAY BREVITIES, 1941

57. YOU SAID A MOUTHFUL, 1932

58. HAUNTED GOLD, 1932

59. ILLEGAL, 1932

60. LOVE IS A RACKET, 1932

61. TAXI, 1932, title card

62. THE TENDERFOOT, 1932, title card

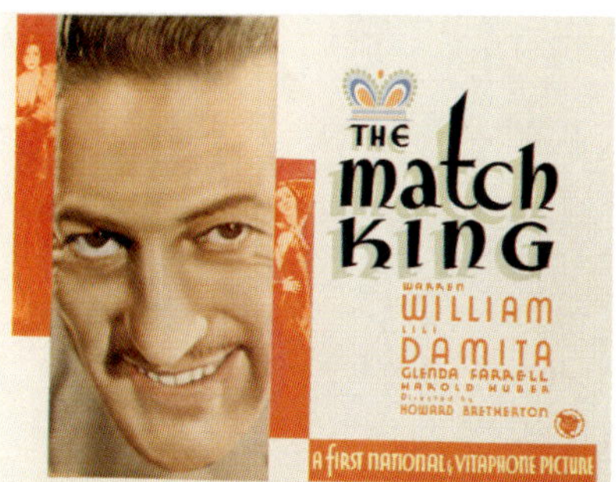

63. THE MATCH KING, 1932, title card

64. 42ND STREET, 1933

65. 42ND STREET, 1933

66. THE PURCHASE PRICE, 1932

67. 42ND STREET, 1933

68. SPORTSLANTS, 1933

69. THE ST LOUIS KID, 1934

70. SEE AMERICA FIRST, 1934

71. THE MAN WITH TWO FACES, 1934

72. WONDER BAR, 1934

73. AS THE EARTH TURNS, 1934

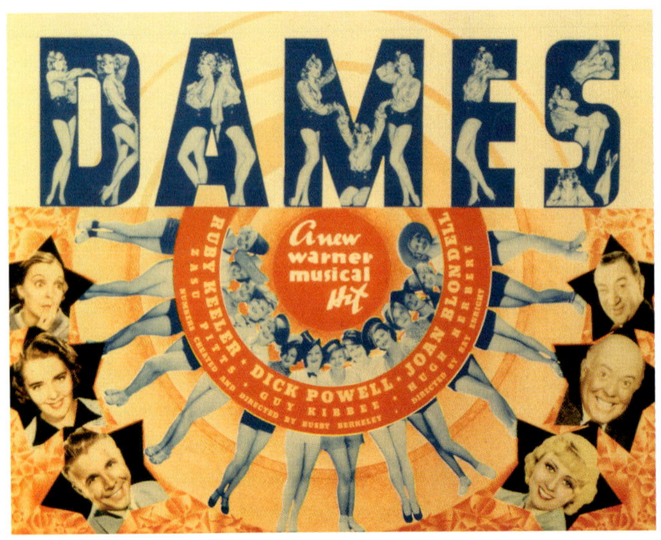

74. DAMES, 1934, title card

75. FASHIONS OF 1934, 1934, title card

76. 6 DAY BIKE RIDER, 1934

77. HAROLD TEEN, 1934

78. THE KEY, 1934

79. BIG HEARTED HERBERT, 1934

80. MYSTERY OF THE WAX MUSEUM, 1935

81. TRAVELING SALESLADY, 1935, Swedish

82. GO INTO YOUR DANCE, 1935, title card

83. CAPTAIN BLOOD, 1935

84. BORDERTOWN, c.1930s re-release, one-sheet

85. IN CALIENTE, 1935, Swedish

86. IN CALIENTE, 1935, title card

87. I FOUND STELLA PARISH, 1935, title card

88. THE IRISH IN US, 1935

89. I FOUND STELLA PARISH, 1935, Swedish

90. MELODY MASTER BANDS, 1936

91. LONESOME TRAILER, 1936

92. ECHO MOUNTAIN, 1936

93. DOWN THE STRETCH, 1936

94. CHINA CLIPPER, 1936

95. CHINA CLIPPER, 1936, Swedish

96. ANTHONY ADVERSE, 1936

97. HEARTS DIVIDED, 1936, window card

98. THREE MEN ON A HORSE, 1936, insert

99. I MARRIED A DOCTOR, 1936

100. THE PETRIFIED FOREST, 1936

101. THE CHARGE OF THE LIGHT BRIGADE, 1936, title card

102. JAILBREAK, 1936, title card

103. THE WHITE ANGEL, 1936, title card

104. PUBLIC ENEMY'S WIFE, 1936, title card

105. GIVE ME YOUR HEART, 1936

106. THE GREEN PASTURES, 1936

107. BRIDES ARE LIKE THAT, 1936, title card

108. BULLETS OR BALLOTS, 1936

109. MOUNTAIN JUSTICE, 1937, title card

110. MISSING WITNESSES, 1937, title card

111. IT'S LOVE I'M AFTER, 1937

112. GUNS OF THE PECOS, 1937, title card

113. FLY-AWAY BABY, 1937, title card

114. EXPENSIVE HUSBANDS, 1937, title card

115. LOVE IS ON THE AIR, 1937

116. OVER THE GOAL, 1937, title card

117. GREEN LIGHT, 1937, title card

118. THE SINGING MARINE, 1937, title card

119. THAT CERTAIN WOMAN, 1937

120. VARSITY SHOW, 1937

121. THE PRINCE AND THE PAUPER, 1949 re-release, one-sheet

122. THE LIFE OF EMILE ZOLA, 1937, window card

123. READY, WILLING AND ABLE, 1937, title card

124. THE ADVENTUROUS BLONDE, 1937

125. THE PERFECT SPECIMEN, 1937

126. PENROD AND SAM, 1937, title card

127. THE DAWN PATROL, 1938

128. FOOLS FOR SCANDAL, 1938, title card

129. RACKET BUSTERS, 1938, title card

130. SERGEANT MURPHY, 1938

131. ANGELS WITH DIRTY FACES, 1938

132. SWING YOUR LADY, 1938, title card

133. WOMEN ARE LIKE THAT, 1938, title card

134. THE ADVENTURES OF ROBIN HOOD, 1938

135. THE ADVENTURES OF ROBIN HOOD, 1938

136. BLONDES AT WORK, 1938, title card

137. CRIME SCHOOL, 1938, title card

138. ACCIDENTS WILL HAPPEN, 1938, title card

139. OVER THE WALL, 1938, title card

140. BROTHER RAT, 1938, title card

141. THE ADVENTURES OF ROBIN HOOD, 1951 re-release, Danish

142. SERGEANT MURPHY, 1938

145. THE SISTERS, 1938

143. A SLIGHT CASE OF MURDER, 1938

144. BOY MEETS GIRL, 1938, window card

146. BROTHER RAT, c.1940s re-release, one-sheet

147. GOLD DIGGERS IN PARIS, 1938, window card

148. THE INVISIBLE MENACE, 1938, window card

149. THE PRIVATE LIVES OF ELIZABETH AND ESSEX, 1939, title card

150. THEY MADE ME A CRIMINAL, 1939, title card

151. YOU CAN'T GET AWAY WITH MURDER, 1939

152. SWEEPSTAKES WINNER, 1939, title card

153. TORCHY PLAYS WITH DYNAMITE, 1939, title card

154. ON YOUR TOES, 1939, title card

155. ESPIONAGE AGENT, 1939, title card

156. GRANNY GET YOUR GUN, 1939, title card

157. WOMEN IN THE WIND, 1939, title card

158. YES MY DARLING DAUGHTER, 1939, title card

159. DEVIL'S ISLAND, 1939, title card

160. THE OKLAHOMA KID, 1939

161. CODE OF THE SECRET SERVICE, 1939

162. COWBOY QUARTERBACK, 1939, title card

163. FOUR WIVES, 1939, title card

164. THE KID FROM KOKOMO, 1939, title card

165. KING OF THE UNDERWORLD, 1939

166. INVISIBLE STRIPES, 1939, title card

167. DODGE CITY, 1939

168. ANGELS WASH THEIR FACES, 1939

169. EACH DAWN I DIE, 1939

170. DUST BE MY DESTINY, 1939, Swedish

171. INDIANAPOLIS SPEEDWAY, 1939, Swedish

172. THE ON DRESS PARADE, 1939

173. THE ADVENTURES OF JANE ARDEN, 1939

174. HELL'S KITCHEN, 1939

175. HELL'S KITCHEN, 1939, Swedish

176. SEEING RED, 1939

177. BROTHER RAT AND A BABY, 1940, title card

178. CITY FOR CONQUEST, 1940

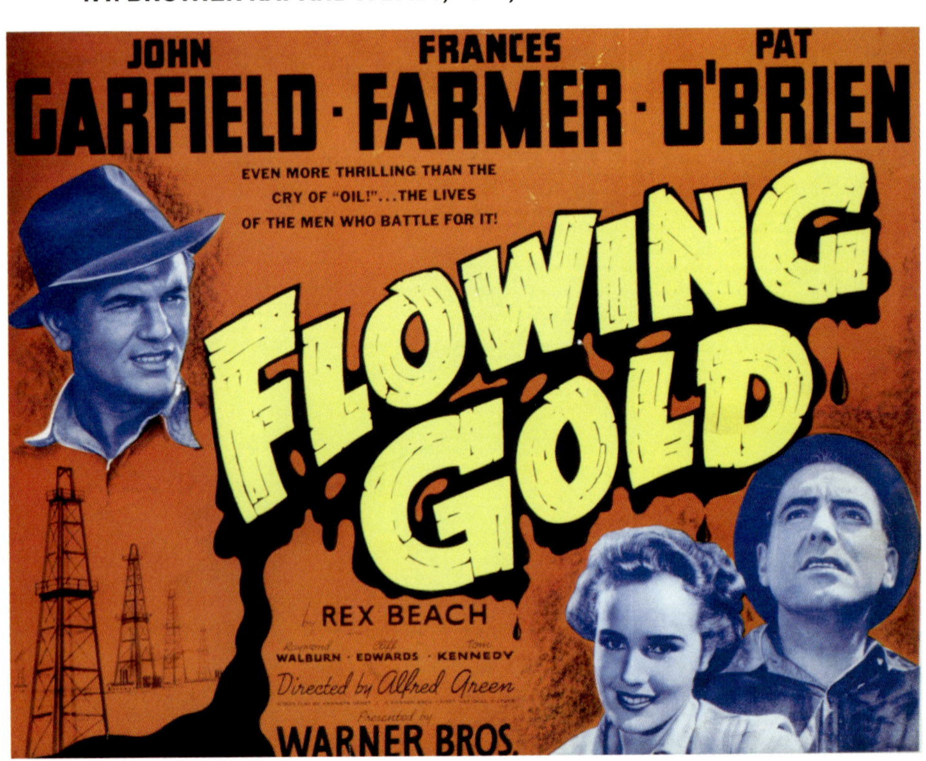

179. FLOWING GOLD, 1940, title card

180. TEDDY THE ROUGH RIDER, 1946
re-release, one-sheet

181. KING OF THE LUMBERJACKS, 1940

182. YOUNG AMERICA FLIES, 1940

183. SERVICE WITH THE COLORS, 1940

184. HOLLYWOOD NOVELTIES, 1940

185. SANTA FE TRAIL, 1940

GEORGE RAFT · ANN SHERIDAN · IDA LUPINO · HUMPHREY BOGART
THEY DRIVE BY NIGHT
WARNER BROS.

186. THEY DRIVE BY NIGHT, 1940, 8 lobby cards

187. NO TIME FOR COMEDY, 1940

188. CITY FOR CONQUEST, 1940, Swedish

189. SATURDAY'S CHILDREN, 1940

190. BROTHER ORCHID, 1940

191. MURDER IN THE AIR, 1940, title card

192. SANTA FE TRAIL, 1940

193. THE SEA HAWK, 1940, title card

194. THREE CHEERS FOR THE IRISH, 1940, title card

195. SATURDAY'S CHILDREN, 1940, title card

196. DISPATCH FROM REUTERS, 1940, title card

197. TORRID ZONE, 1940, title card

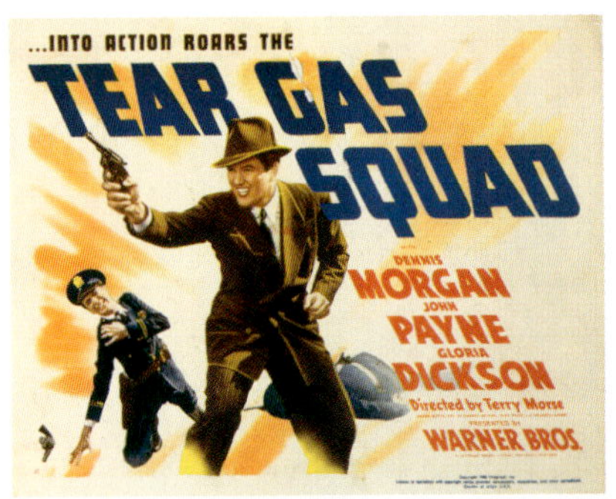

198. TEAR GAS SQUAD, 1940, title card

199. CALLING PHILO VANCE, 1940, title card

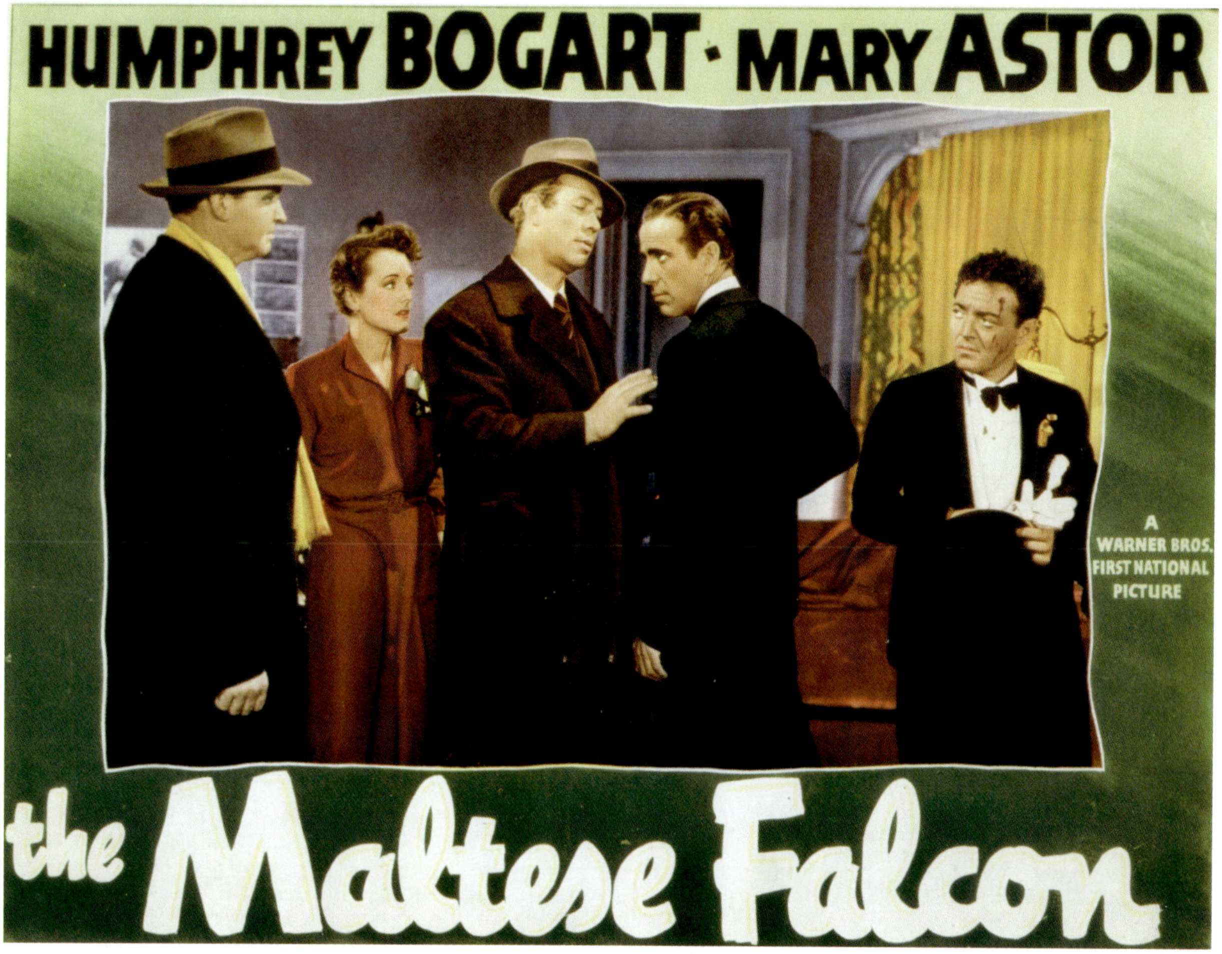
HUMPHREY BOGART · MARY ASTOR
A
WARNER BROS.
FIRST NATIONAL
PICTURE
the Maltese Falcon
200. THE MALTESE FALCON, 1941

HUMPHREY BOGART · MARY ASTOR
A
WARNER BROS.
FIRST NATIONAL
PICTURE
the Maltese Falcon
201. THE MALTESE FALCON, 1941

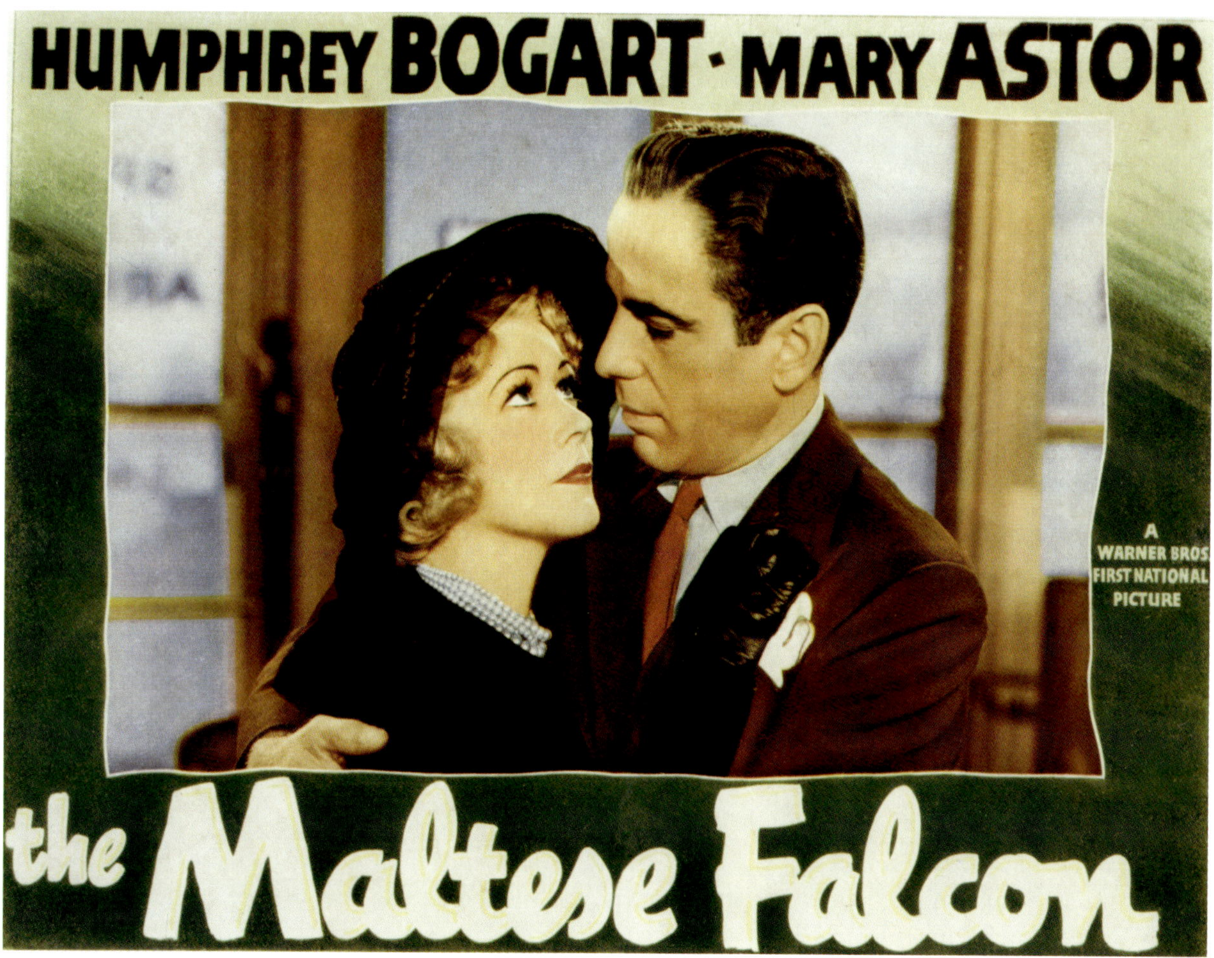

202. HIGH SIERRA, 1941

203. THEY DIED WITH THEIR BOOTS ON, 1941, title card

204. MEET JOHN DOE, 1941, title card

205. THE STRAWBERRY BLONDE, 1941, title card

206. THE BRIDE CAME C.O.D., 1941, title card

207. NINE LIVES ARE NOT ENOUGH, 1941, title card

208. SERGEANT YORK, 1941, title card

209. INTERNATIONAL SQUADRON, 1941, title card

210. OUT OF THE FOG, 1941, title card

211. MANPOWER, 1941, title card

212. THE CASE OF THE BLACK PARROT, 1941

213. MILLION DOLLAR BABY, 1941

214. ONE FOOT IN HEAVEN, 1941

215. SPORTS PARADE, 1941

216. THE WAGONS ROLL AT NIGHT, 1941

217. THE SMILING GHOST, 1941

218. THE RETURN OF DOCTOR X, 1939

219. STARDUST, 1941

220. TARGET FOR TONIGHT, 1941

221. THIEVES FALL OUT, 1941

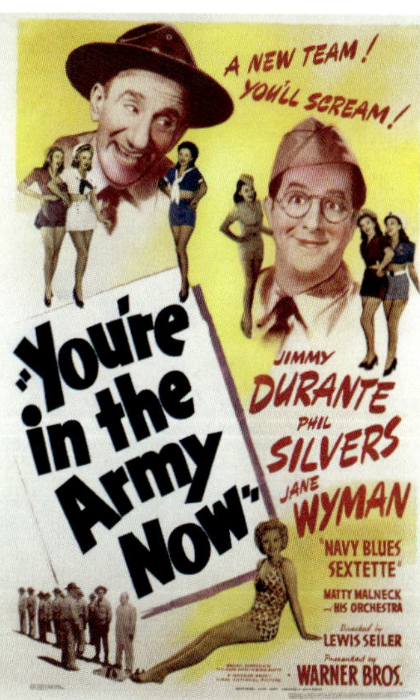

222. YOU'RE IN THE ARMY NOW, 1941

223. CASABLANCA, 1942

224. THE BIG SHOT, 1942, half-sheet

225. CASABLANCA, 1942, Australian daybill

226. NOW VOYAGER, 1942, title card and scene lobby card

227. ALL THROUGH THE NIGHT, 1942, insert

228. SECRET ENEMIES, 1942

229. CAPTAINS OF THE CLOUDS, 1942, title card

230. LARCENY INC, 1942, half-sheet

231. DANGEROUSLY THEY LIVE, 1942, title card

232. THE MAN WHO CAME TO DINNER, 1942

233. LARCENY INC, 1942

234. GEORGE WASHINGTON SLEPT HERE, 1942, title card

235. YANKEE DOODLE DANDY, 1942, title card

236. JUKE GIRL, 1942, title card

237. KINGS ROW, 1942, title card

238. GENTLEMAN JIM, 1942, title card

239. ACTION IN THE NORTH ATLANTIC, 1943, title card

240. THANK YOUR LUCKY STARS, 1943, title card

241. DESTINATION TOKYO, 1943

242. WATCH ON THE RHINE, 1943

243. BETTE DAVIS, 1943, personality poster

244. ARSENIC AND OLD LACE, 1944

245. TO HAVE AND HAVE NOT, 1944, title card

246. PASSAGE TO MARSEILLE, 1944, title card

247. ROAD TO VICTORY, 1944

248. SHINE ON HARVEST MOON, 1944, title card

249. CONFLICT, 1945

250. PRIDE OF THE MARINES, 1945, title card

251. SAN ANTONIO, 1945

252. MILDRED PIERCE, 1945, insert

253. THE HORN BLOWS AT MIDNIGHT, 1945, insert

254. CHRISTMAS IN CONNECTICUT, 1945

255. SARATOGA TRUNK, 1945, insert

256. TOO YOUNG TO KNOW, 1945, insert

257. THE HORN BLOWS AT MIDNIGHT, 1945, title card

258. CONFIDENTIAL AGENT, 1945, title card

259. THE BIG SLEEP, 1946

260. MY REPUTATION, 1946, title card

261. NEVER SAY GOODBYE, 1946, half-sheet

262. NIGHT AND DAY, 1946, title card

263. CLOAK AND DAGGER, 1946, title card

264. DECEPTION, 1946, title card

265. NOBODY LIVES FOREVER, 1946, title card

266. THE STOLEN LIFE, 1946, title card

267. THREE STRANGERS, 1946, half-sheet

268. RHAPSODY IN BLUE, 1946, title card

269. DARK PASSAGE, 1947

270. THAT HAGEN GIRL, 1947, title card

271. CRY WOLF, 1947, half-sheet

272. THE TWO MRS CARROLLS, 1947, title card

273. STALLION ROAD, 1947, title card

274. BEAST WITH FIVE FINGERS, 1947, title card

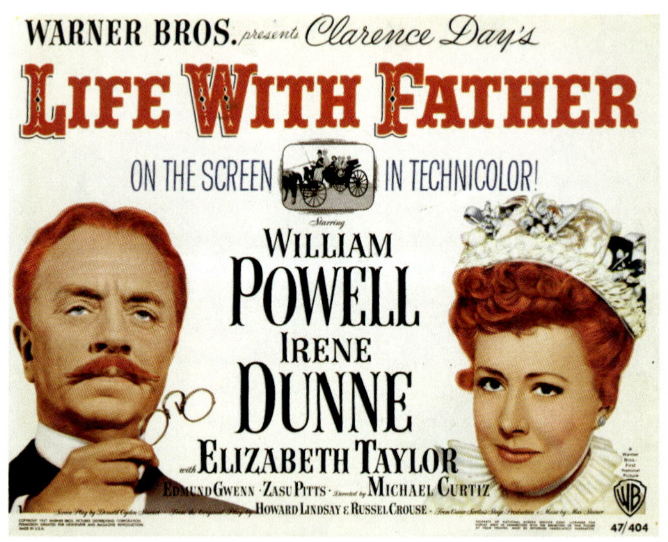

275. LIFE WITH FATHER, 1947, title card

276. KEY LARGO, 1948, title card

277. ESCAPE ME NEVER, 1948, title card

278. ROPE, 1948, title card

279. ROMANCE ON THE HIGH SEAS, 1948, title card

280. THE TREASURE OF THE SIERRA MADRE, 1948, title card

281. THE TREASURE OF THE SIERRA MADRE, 1948

282. THE VOICE OF THE TURTLE, 1948, title card

283. APRIL SHOWERS, 1948

284. I BECAME A CRIMINAL, 1948

285. JOHNNY BELINDA, 1948

286. JUNE BRIDE, 1948

287. SMART GIRLS DON'T TALK, 1948

288. A WARNER BROTHERS CARTOON, 1948

289. EMBRACEABLE YOU, 1948

290. MY WILD IRISH ROSE, 1948

291. TWO GUYS FROM TEXAS, 1948

292. WINTER MEETING, 1948

293. WOMAN IN WHITE, 1948

294. WHITE HEAT, 1949, title card

295. ADVENTURES OF DON JUAN, 1949, title card

296. THE GIRL FROM JONES BEACH, 1949, title card

297. FLAMINGO ROAD, 1949, title card

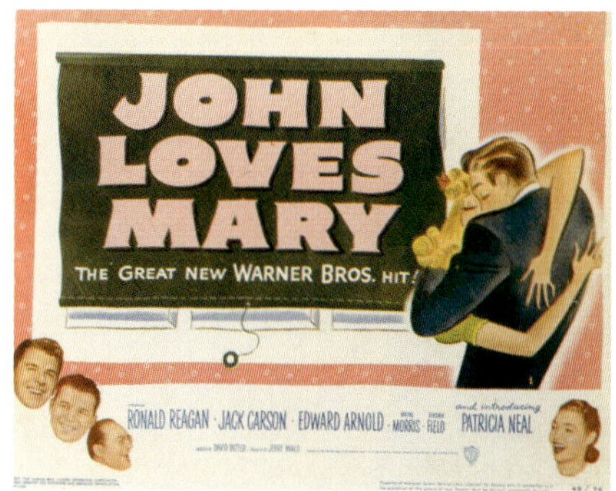

298. JOHN LOVES MARY, 1949, title card

299. LOOK FOR THE SILVER LINING, 1949, title card

300. THE FOUNTAINHEAD, 1949, title card

301. MY DREAM IS YOURS, 1949, title card

302. UNDER CAPRICORN, 1949, title card

303. THE FOUNTAINHEAD, 1949

304. KISS TOMORROW GOODBYE, 1950, title card

305. YOUNG MAN WITH A HORN, 1950, title card

306. TEA FOR TWO, 1950, title card

307. THE DAMNED DON'T CRY, 1950, title card

308. THE WEST POINT STORY, 1950, title card

309. THE INSPECTOR GENERAL, 1950, title card

310. HASTY HEART, 1950, title card

311. THE FLAME AND THE ARROW, 1950, title card

312. BACKFIRE, 1950, title card

313. GLASS MENAGERIE, 1950, title card

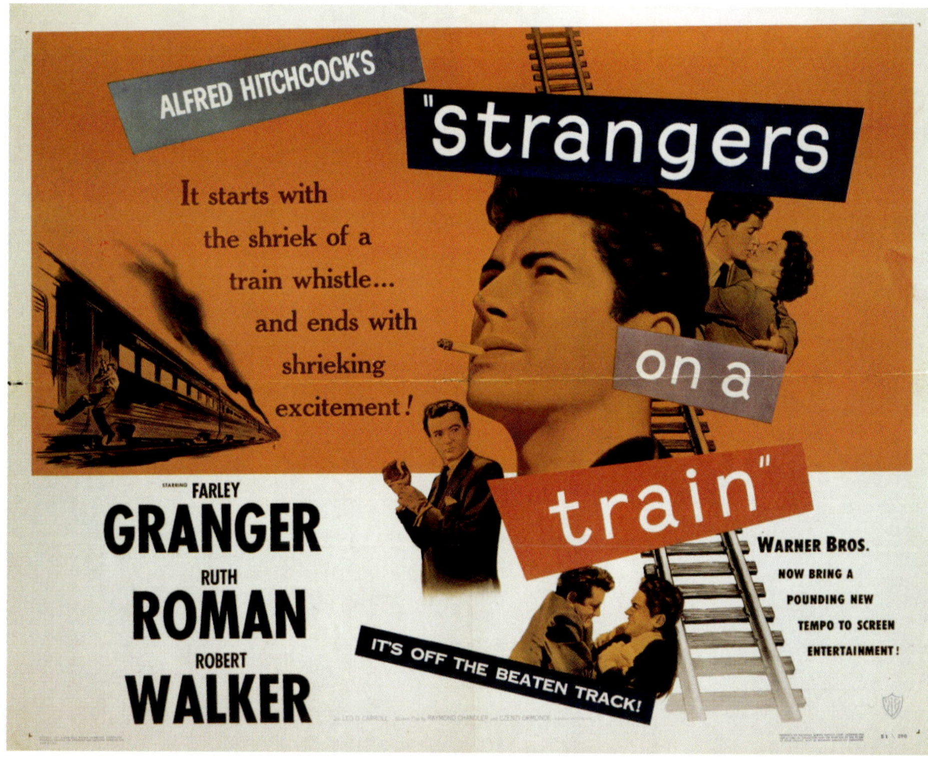

314. STRANGERS ON A TRAIN, 1951, half-sheet

315. HIGHWAY 301, 1951

316. SUGARFOOT, 1951, title card

317. THE ENFORCER, 1951, title card

318. LIGHTNING STRIKES TWICE, 1951, title card

319. A STREETCAR NAMED DESIRE,
1958 re-release, title card

320. LULLABY OF BROADWAY, 1951, title card

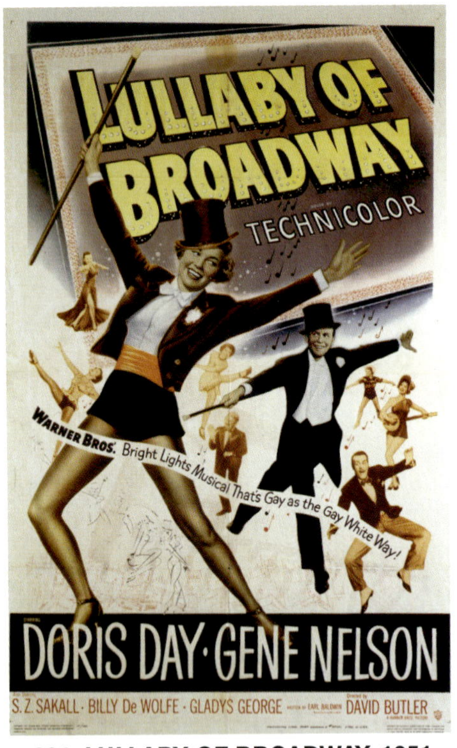

321. LULLABY OF BROADWAY, 1951

322. OPERATION PACIFIC, 1951

323. STORM WARNING, 1951

324. ALONG THE GREAT DIVIDE, 1951

325. CAPTAIN HORATIO HORNBLOWER, 1951

326. COME FILL THE CUP, 1951

327. INSIDE THE WALLS OF FOLSOM PRISON, 1951

328. JIM THORPE ALL AMERICAN, 1951, insert

329. ON MOONLIGHT BAY, 1951

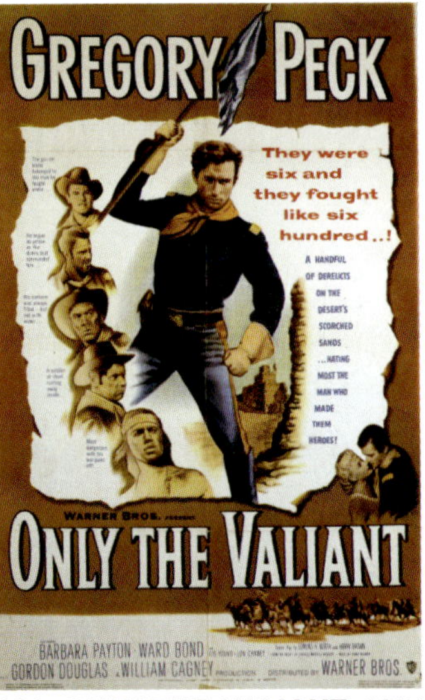

330. ONLY THE VALIANT, 1951

331. TOMORROW IS ANOTHER DAY, 1951

332. I'LL SEE YOU IN MY DREAMS, 1952

333. 3 FOR BEDROOM C, 1952, half-sheet

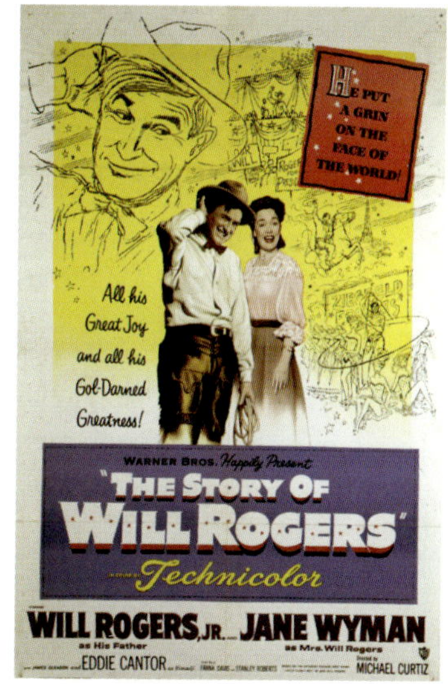

334. THE STORY OF WILL ROGERS, 1952

335. SHE'S WORKING HER WAY THROUGH COLLEGE, 1952

336. THE SAN FRANCISCO STORY, 1952

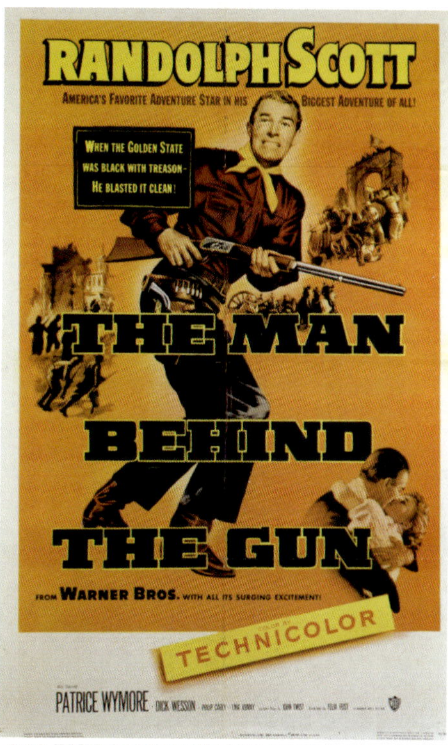

337. THE MAN BEHIND THE GUN, 1952

338. WHERE'S CHARLEY, 1952

339. RETREAT HELL, 1952

340. JACK & THE BEANSTALK, 1952

341. OPERATION SECRET, 1952

342. THE MOONLIGHTER, 1953, half-sheet

WARNER BROS. PRESENT
"So This is Love"
TECHNICOLOR
WHEN SHE SHIMMIED, THE SHOW-WORLD SHOOK! WHEN SHE SANG, THE WHOLE WORLD THRILLED!
Marvelous Music!
THE STORY OF GRACE MOORE
KATHRYN GRAYSON

343. SO THIS IS LOVE, 1953

344. HOUSE OF WAX, 1953, three-sheet

345. I CONFESS, 1953, three-sheet

346. TROUBLE ALONG THE WAY, 1953, three-sheet

347. THE BEAST FROM 20,000 FATHOMS, 1953

348. THE BEAST FROM 20,000 FATHOMS, 1953, 8 lobby cards

349. SHE'S BACK ON BROADWAY, 1953, half-sheet

350. THE JAZZ SINGER, 1953

351. A STAR IS BORN, 1954, Argentinean two-sheet

352. 3 SAILORS & A GIRL, 1954

353. A STAR IS BORN, 1954, 8 lobby cards

354. PHANTOM OF THE RUE MORGUE, 1954, three-sheet

355. REBEL WITHOUT A CAUSE, 1955

356. REBEL WITHOUT A CAUSE, 1955, 8 lobby cards

357. REBEL WITHOUT A CAUSE, 1955, British quad

358. THE SILVER CHALICE, 1955

359. EAST OF EDEN, 1955, half-sheet

THE MILLION-DOLLAR KILLER AND THE DIME-A-DANCE DOLL...
THE STORY BEHIND THE TERRIFYING 60-DAY HUNT FOR DESPERADO 'MAD-DOG' EARLE!
"I died a thousand times"
CINEMASCOPE
JACK PALANCE
SHELLEY WINTERS
WARNER BROS. LORI NELSON · LEE MARVIN · GONZALEZ GONZALEZ

360. I DIED A 1000 TIMES, 1955

361. MISTER ROBERTS, 1955

362. MISTER ROBERTS, 1955, 8 lobby cards

363. THE LONE RANGER, 1956

364. THE SEARCHERS, 1956

365. THE BAD SEED, 1956

366. CHASING THE SUN, 1956

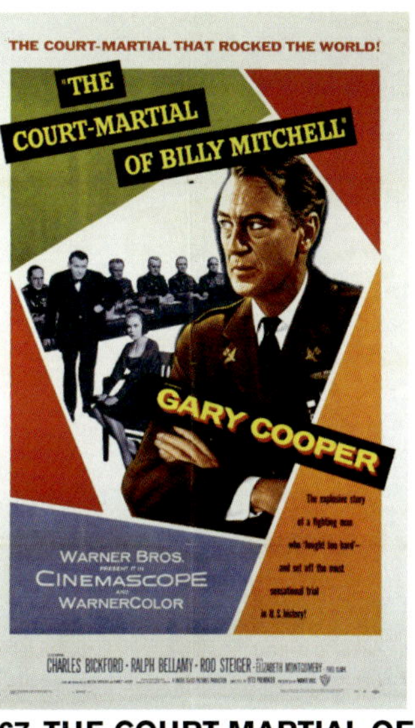

367. THE COURT-MARTIAL OF BILLY MITCHELL, 1956

368. OUR MISS BROOKS, 1956

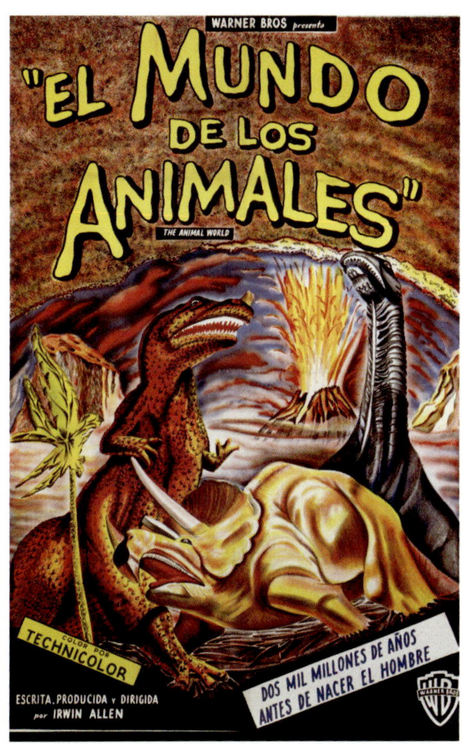

369. THE ANIMAL WORLD, 1956, Argentinean

370. GIANT, 1956, 40x60

371. MOBY DICK, 1956

372. TOP SECRET AFFAIR, 1957

373. THE STORY OF MANKIND, 1957, title card

374. THE HELEN MORGAN STORY, 1957

375. THE PRINCE & THE SHOWGIRL, 1957

376. THE JAMES DEAN STORY, 1957, insert

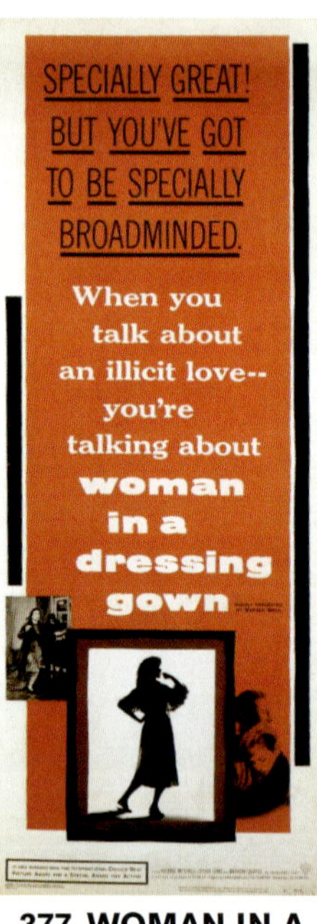

377. WOMAN IN A DRESSING GOWN, 1957, insert

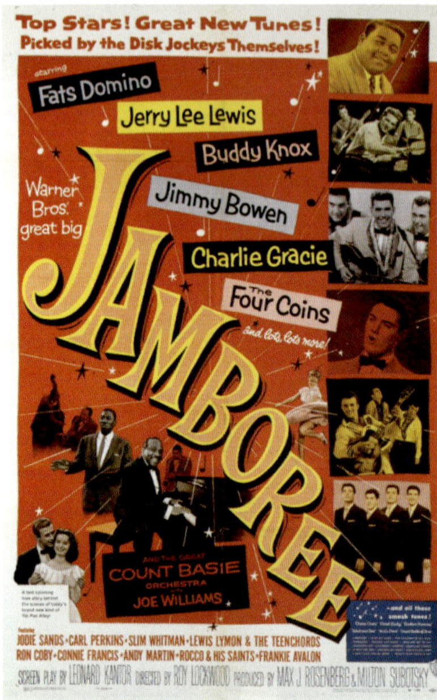

378. JAMBOREE, 1957

379. THE PAJAMA GAME, 1957, half-sheet

380. A FACE IN THE CROWD, 1957, half-sheet

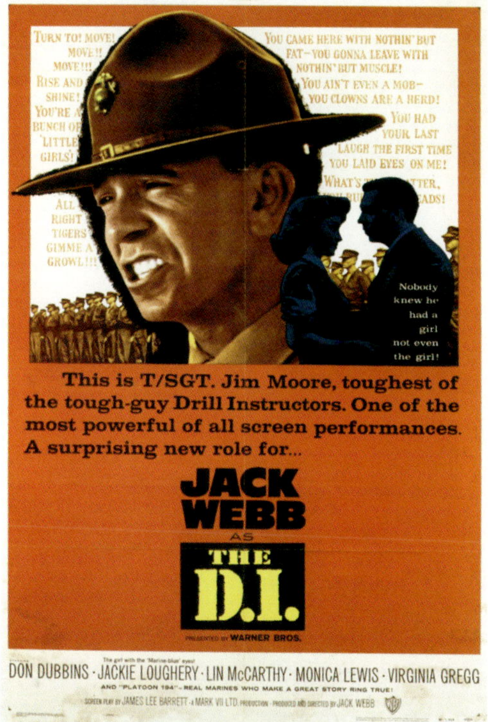

381. THE DI, 1957

382. THE BIG LAND, 1957

383. THE GREEN-EYED BLONDE, 1957

384. INDISCREET, 1958

385. MARJORIE MORNINGSTAR, 1958

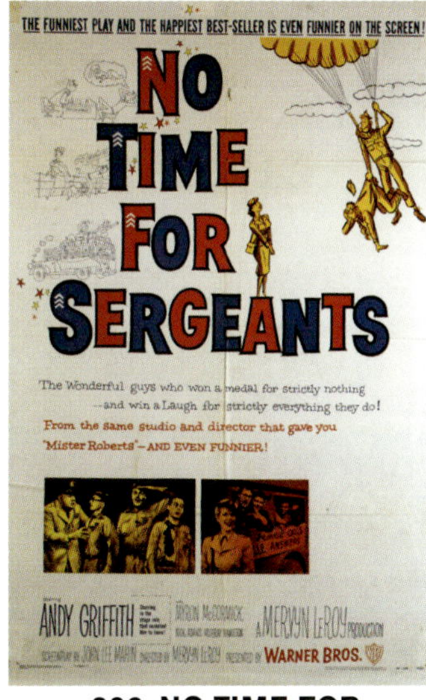

386. NO TIME FOR SERGEANTS, 1958

387. THE DEEP SIX, 1958

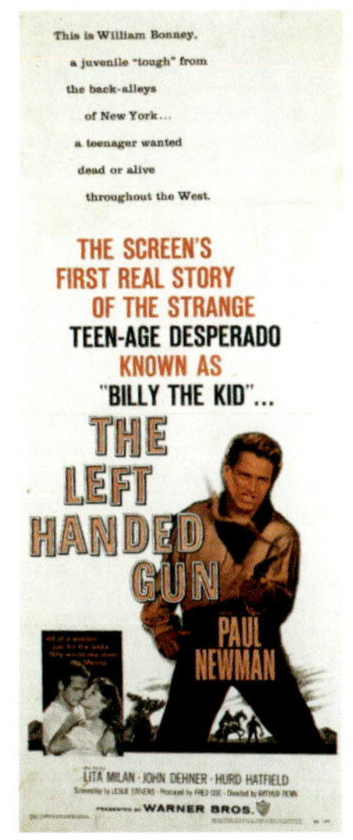

388. THE LEFT HANDED GUN, 1958, insert

389. OLD MAN & THE SEA, 1958, Italian two-panel

390. STAKEOUT ON DOPE STREET, 1958

391. WIND ACROSS THE EVERGLADES, 1958

392. THE NUN'S STORY, 1959

393. RIO BRAVO, 1959

394. BORN RECKLESS, 1959, three-sheet

395. GIGANTIS THE FIRE MONSTER, 1959, insert

396. TEENAGERS FROM OUTER SPACE, 1959

397. THE FBI STORY, 1959

398. A SUMMER PLACE, 1959

399. THE YOUNG PHILADELPHIANS, 1959, half-sheet

400. OCEAN'S 11, 1960

401. OCEAN'S 11, 1960, 8 lobby cards

402. GIRL OF THE NIGHT, 1960

403. SUNRISE AT CAMPOBELLO, 1960

404. CASH McCALL, 1960

405. THE SUNDOWNERS, 1961

406. THE SUNDOWNERS, 1961, Italian two-panel

407. CLAUDELLE INGLISH, 1961

408. PORTRAIT OF A MOBSTER, 1961, insert

409. FANNY, 1961

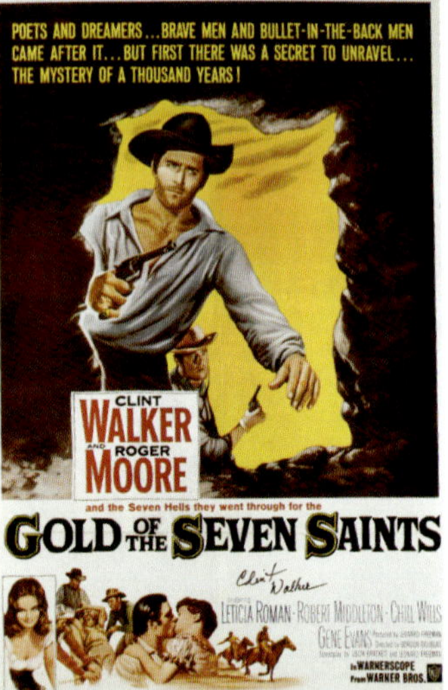

410. GOLD OF THE SEVEN SAINTS, 1961

411. LAD A DOG, 1961

412. FABULOUS WORLD OF JULES VERNE, 1961

413. THE MASK, 1961, half-sheet

414. PARRISH, 1961, insert

415. SPLENDOR IN THE GRASS, 1961, insert

416. GYPSY, 1962, half-sheet

417. THE MUSIC MAN, 1962, British quad

418. THE CHAPMAN REPORT, 1962

419. WHAT EVER HAPPENED TO BABY JANE, 1962, half-sheet

420. GAY PURR-EE, 1962

421. THE SINGER NOT THE SONG, 1962

422. PALM SPRINGS WEEKEND, 1963

423. RAMPAGE, 1963

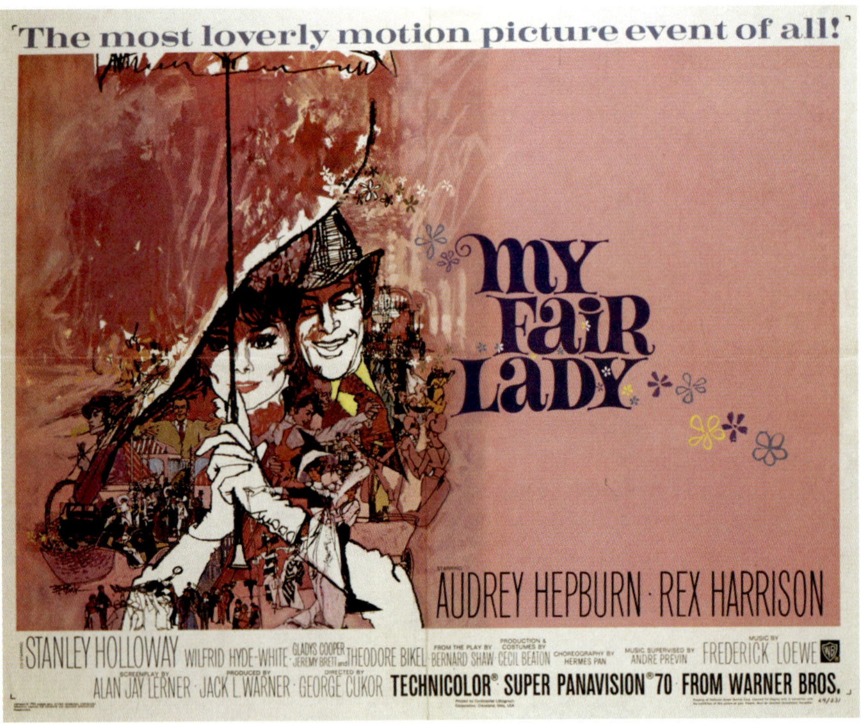

424. MY FAIR LADY, 1964, half-sheet

425. MY FAIR LADY, c.1960s re-release, Italian one-panel

426. KISSES FOR MY PRESIDENT, 1964

427. ROBIN & THE 7 HOODS, 1964, half-sheet

428. THE INCREDIBLE MR. LIMPET, 1964

429. DEAD RINGER, 1964

430. 4 FOR TEXAS, 1964

431. A DISTANT TRUMPET, 1964, half-sheet

432. THE GREAT RACE, 1965

433. HAVING A WILD WEEKEND, 1965

434. HAVING A WILD WEEKEND, 1965

435. A BIG HAND FOR THE LITTLE LADY, 1966

436. ANY WEDNESDAY, 1966

437. CHAMBER OF HORRORS, 1966

438. HARPER, 1966

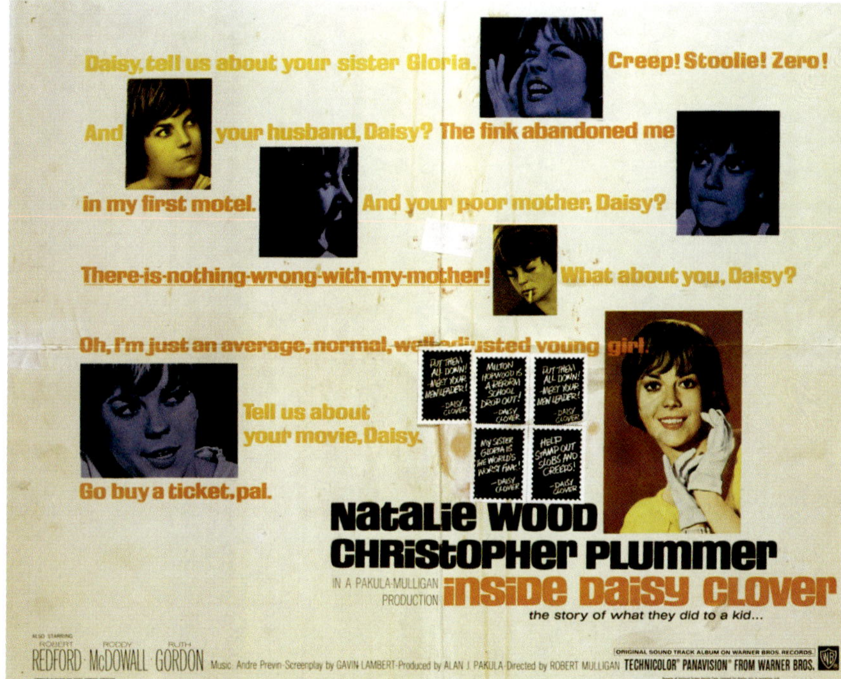

439. INSIDE DAISY CLOVER, 1966, half-sheet

440. WHO'S AFRAID OF VIRGINIA WOOLF, 1966

441. BONNIE AND CLYDE, 1967

442. THE FAMILY WAY, 1967, half-sheet

443. WAIT UNTIL DARK, 1967

444. REFLECTIONS IN A GOLDEN EYE, 1967, half-sheet

445. UP THE DOWN STAIRCASE, 1967, half-sheet

446. COOL HAND LUKE, 1967

447. COOL HAND LUKE, 1967

448. THE GREEN BERETS, 1968

449. FINIAN'S RAINBOW, 1968

450. PETULIA, 1968

451. BULLITT, 1969

452. THE LEARNING TREE, 1969

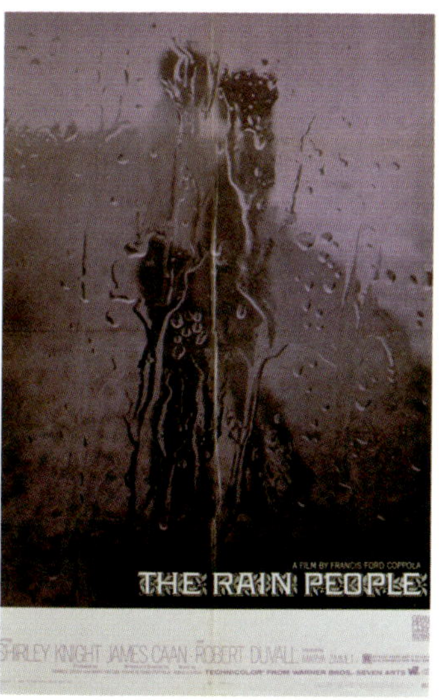

453. THE RAIN PEOPLE, 1969

454. THE WILD BUNCH, 1969

455. FRANKENSTEIN MUST BE DESTROYED, 1970

456. DIRTY HARRY, 1971

457. WHEN DINOSAURS RULED THE EARTH, 1971, door panel

458. DELIVERANCE, 1972

459. CLEOPATRA JONES, 1973

460. JEREMIAH JOHNSON, 1972

461. MAGNUM FORCE, 1973, British quad

462. MEAN STREETS, 1973, Italian photobusta

463. MAGNUM FORCE, 1973

464. ENTER THE DRAGON, 1973

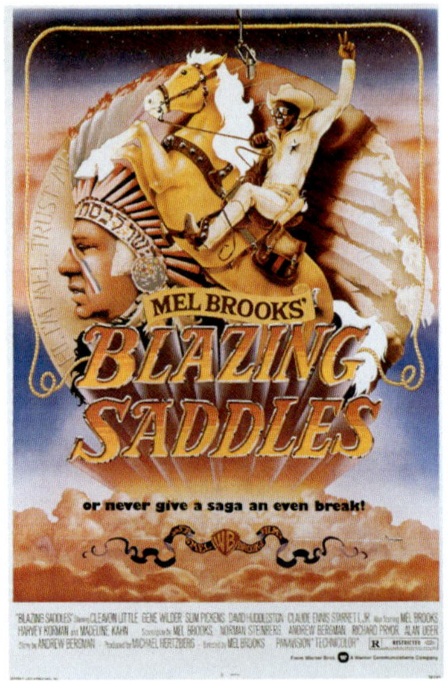

465. BLAZING SADDLES, 1974, 30x40

466. OPERATION DAYBREAK, 1975

467. ALL THE PRESIDENT'S MEN, 1976

468. THE OUTLAW JOSEY WALES, 1976

469. THE OUTLAW JOSEY WALES, 1976, Japanese

470. THE GAUNTLET, 1977

471. THE LATE SHOW, 1977

472. THE SPACE MOVIE, 1979

473. A LITTLE ROMANCE, 1979

474. LIFE OF BRIAN, 1979

475. ALTERED STATES, 1980

476. WHEN TIME RAN OUT, 1980

477. BRONCO BILLY, 1980

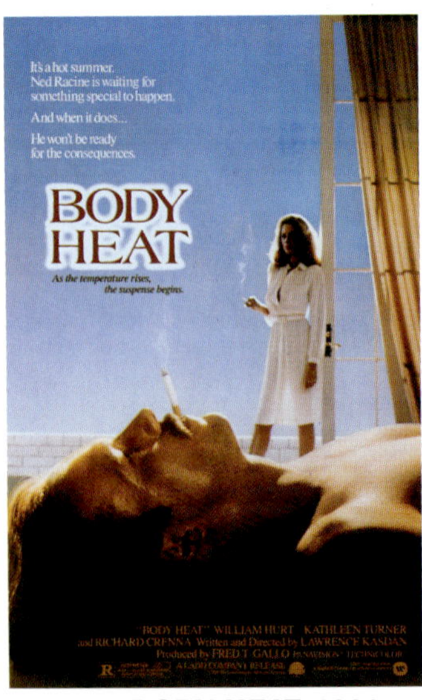

478. BODY HEAT, 1981

479. EXCALIBUR, 1981

480. PRINCE OF THE CITY, 1981

481. PRIVATE BENJAMIN, 1981

482. CREEPSHOW, 1982

483. DEATHTRAP, 1982

484. MAD MAX 2: THE ROAD WARRIOR, 1982

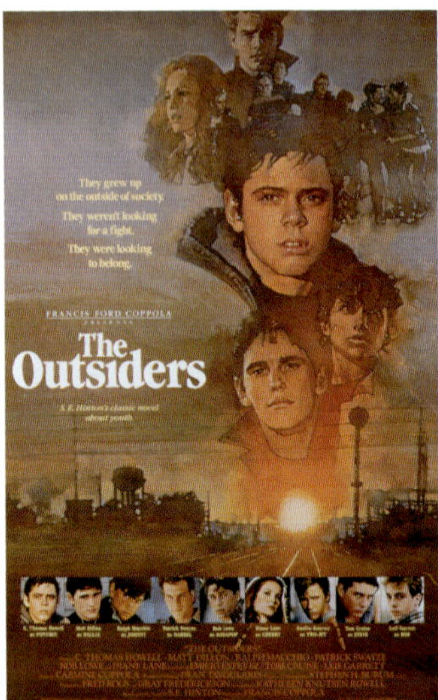

485. OUTSIDERS, 1982

486. THE RIGHT STUFF, 1983

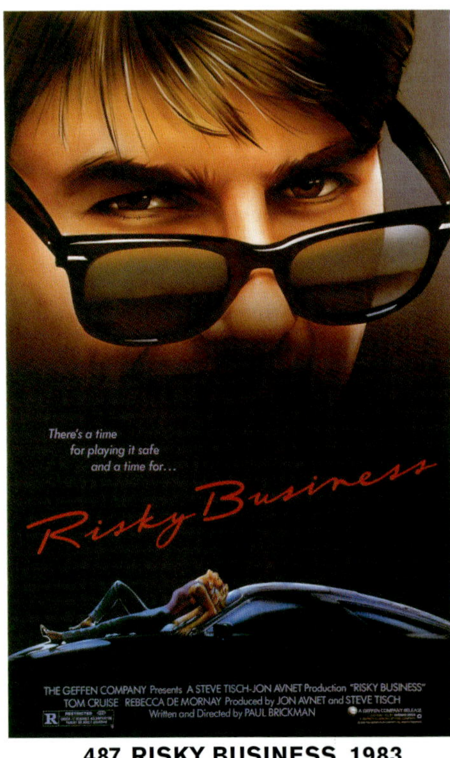

487. RISKY BUSINESS, 1983

488. SUDDEN IMPACT, 1983

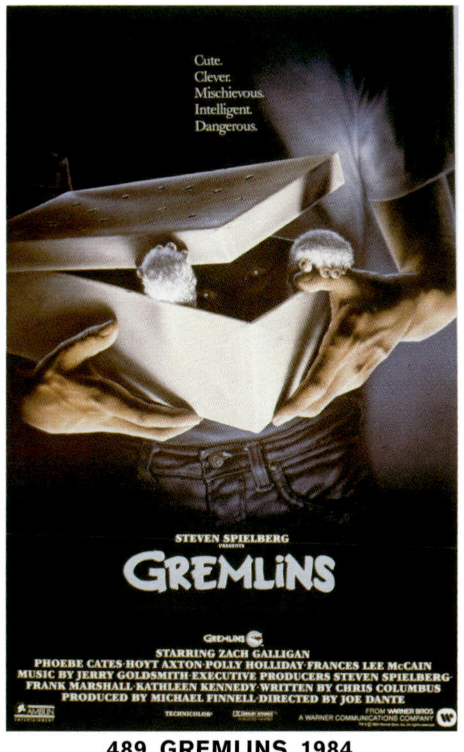

489. GREMLINS, 1984

490. PURPLE RAIN, 1984

491. POLICE ACADEMY, 1984

492. AFTER HOURS, 1985

493. THE COLOR PURPLE, 1985

494. THE GOONIES, 1985

495. PALE RIDER, 1985

496. CLAN OF THE CAVE BEAR, 1986

497. THE MOSQUITO COAST, 1986

498. ROUND MIDNIGHT, 1986

499. UNDER THE CHERRY MOON, 1986

500. FULL METAL JACKET, 1987

501. LETHAL WEAPON, 1987

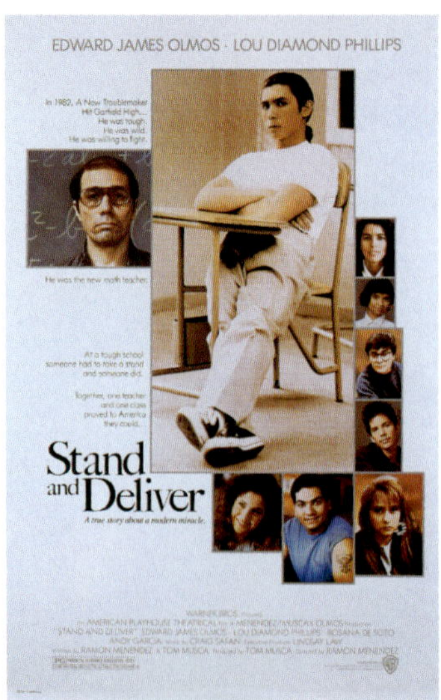

502. STAND AND DELIVER, 1987

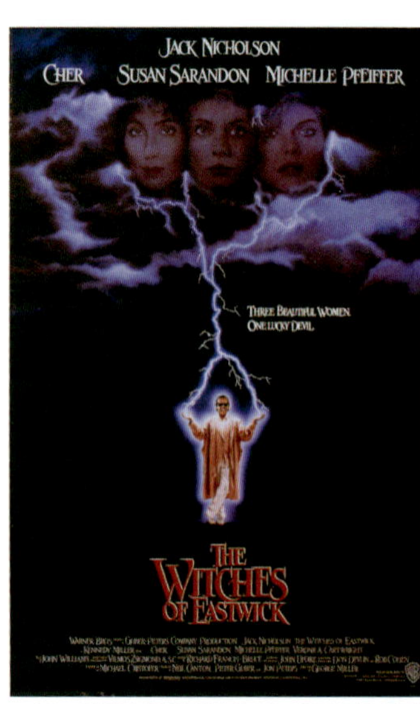

503. THE WITCHES OF EAST-WICK, 1987

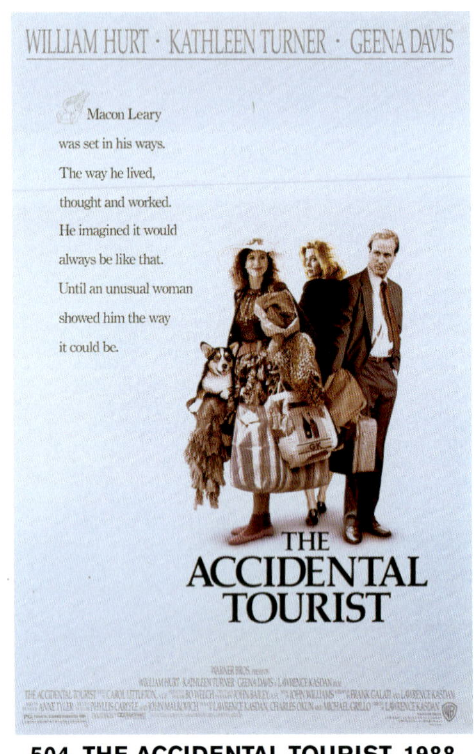

504. THE ACCIDENTAL TOURIST, 1988

505. BEETLEJUICE, 1988

506. IMAGINE, 1988

507. BATMAN, 1989

508. DRIVING MISS DAISY, 1989

509. NATIONAL LAMPOON'S CHRISTMAS VACATION, 1989

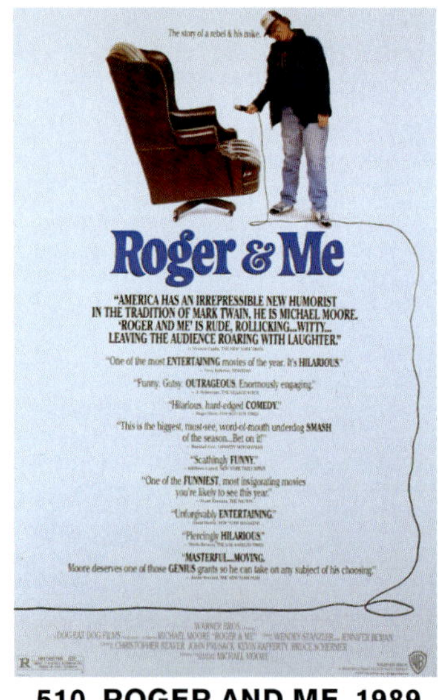

510. ROGER AND ME, 1989

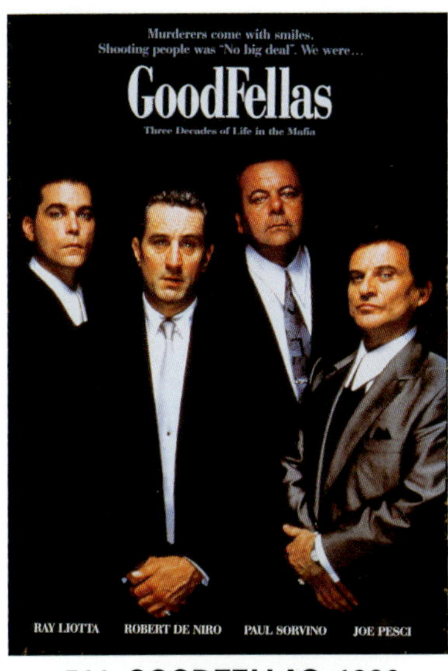

511. GOODFELLAS, 1990

512. HAMLET, 1990

513. IMPULSE, 1990

514. REVERSAL OF FORTUNE, 1990

515. JFK, 1991

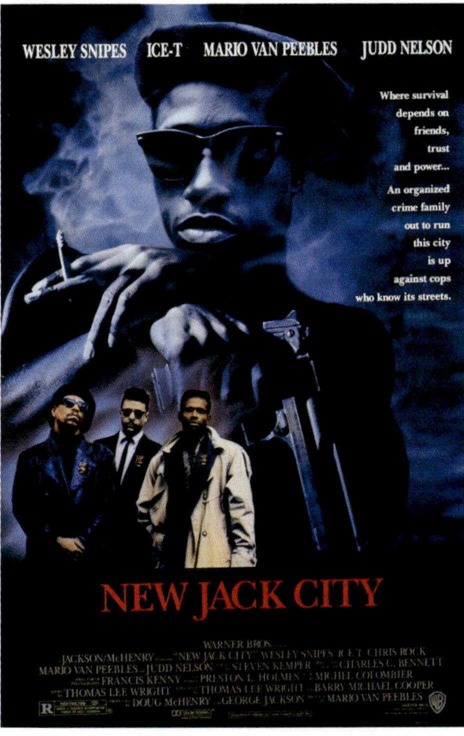

516. NEW JACK CITY, 1991

517. ROBIN HOOD PRINCE OF THIEVES, 1991

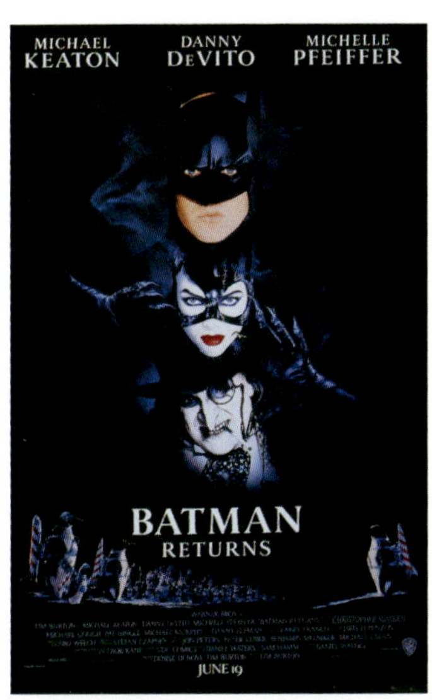

518. BATMAN RETURNS, 1992

519. CLASS ACT, 1992

520. LETHAL WEAPON 3, 1992

521. UNFORGIVEN, 1992

522. THE FUGITIVE, 1993

523. SOMMERSBY, 1993

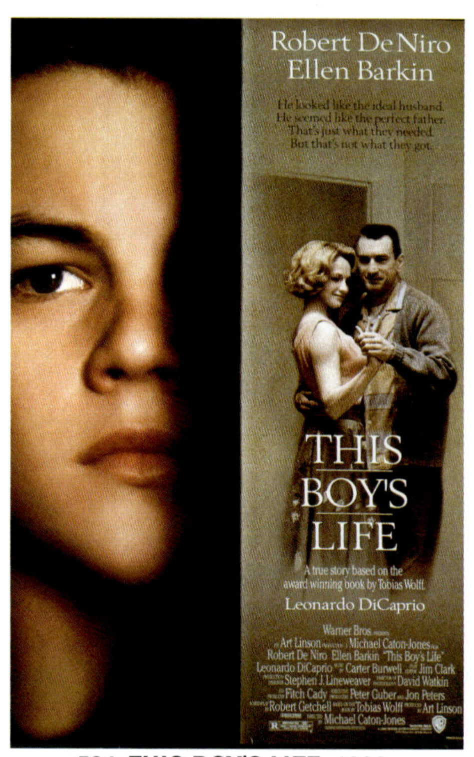

524. THIS BOY'S LIFE, 1993

525. THE HUDSUCKER PROXY, 1994

526. INTERVIEW WITH THE VAMPIRE, 1994

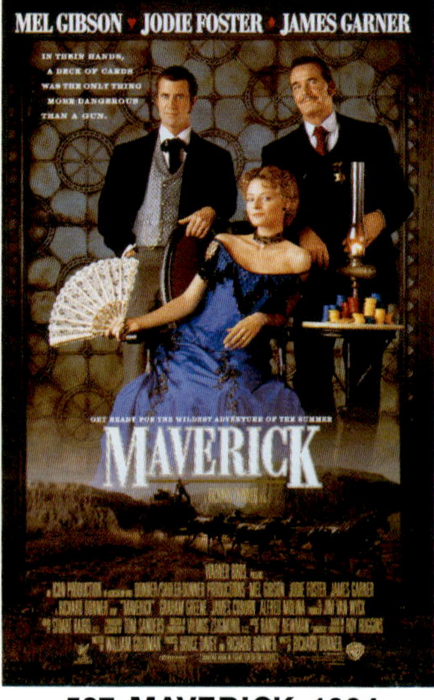

527. MAVERICK, 1994

528. NATURAL BORN KILLERS, 1994

529. ACE VENTURA WHEN NATURE CALLS, 1995

530. THE BRIDGES OF MADISON COUNTY, 1995

531. OUTBREAK, 1995

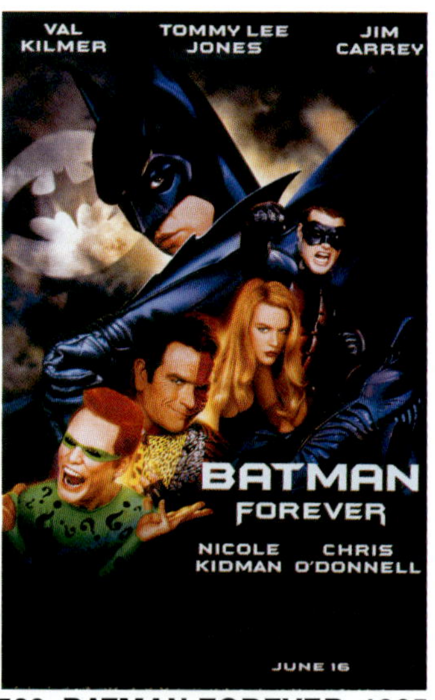

532. BATMAN FOREVER, 1995

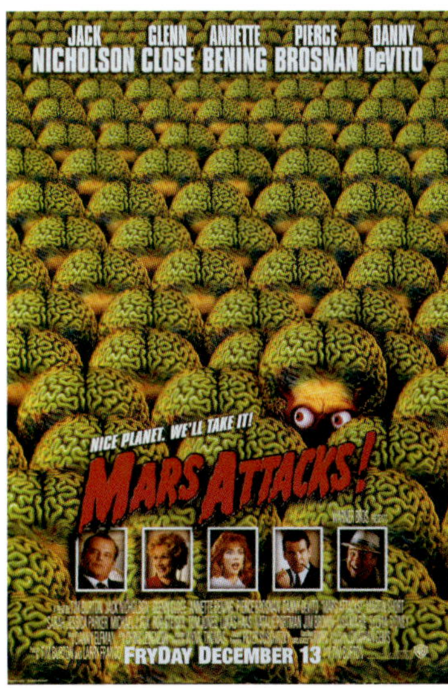

533. MARS ATTACKS, 1996

534. SPACE JAM, 1996

535. TIN CUP, 1996

536. TWISTER, 1996

537. BATMAN AND ROBIN, 1997

538. CONTACT, 1997

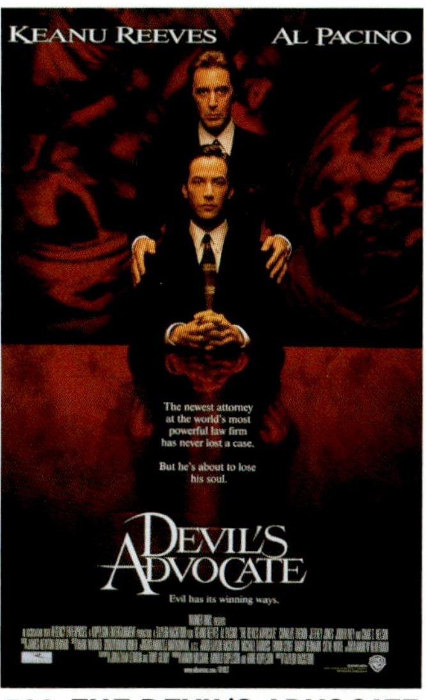

539. THE DEVIL'S ADVOCATE, 1997

540. L.A. CONFIDENTIAL, 1997

541. QUEST FOR CAMELOT, 1998

542. LETHAL WEAPON 4, 1998

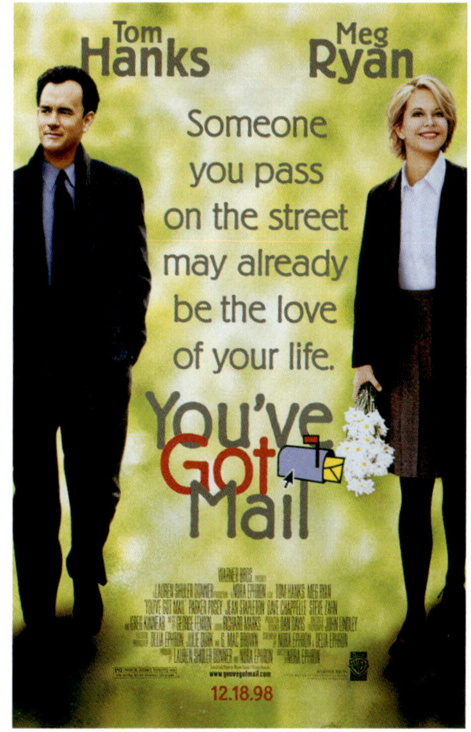

543. YOU'VE GOT MAIL, 1998

544. ANALYZE THIS, 1999

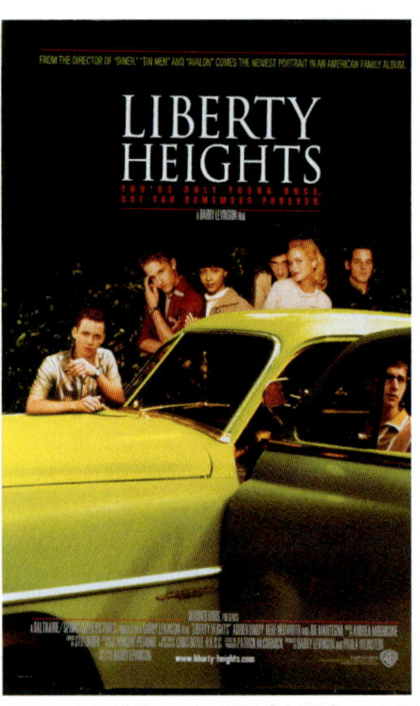

545. LIBERTY HEIGHTS, 1999

546. EYES WIDE SHUT, 1999

547. ANY GIVEN SUNDAY, 1999

548. THE GREEN MILE, 1999

549. THE MATRIX, 1999

550. THE IRON GIANT, 1999

551. BEST IN SHOW, 2000

552. BATTLEFIELD EARTH, 2000

553. GET CARTER, 2000

554. PAY IT FORWARD, 2000

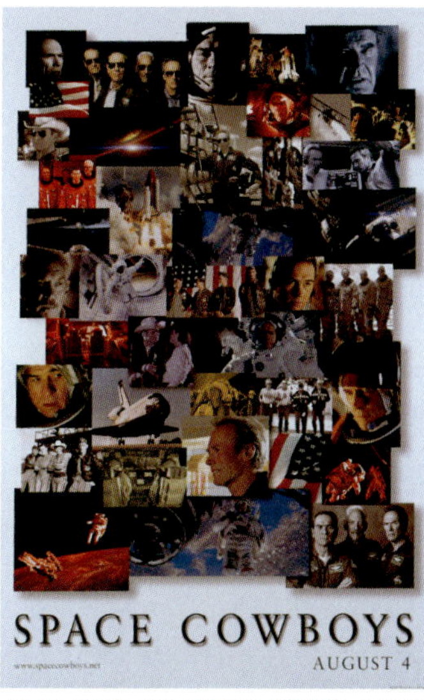

555. SPACE COWBOYS, 2000

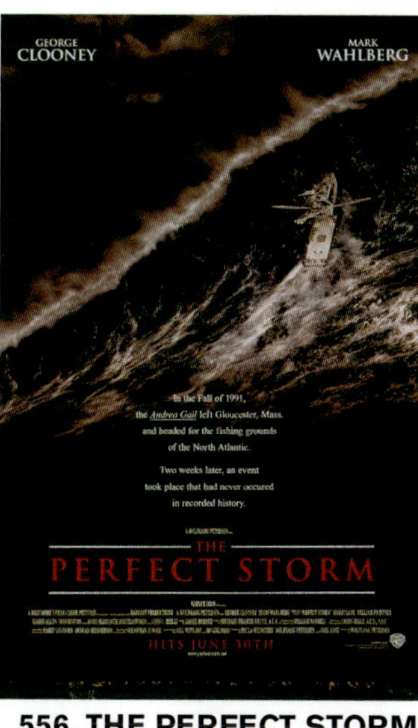

556. THE PERFECT STORM, 2000

557. THE WHOLE NINE YARDS, 2000

558. MISS CONGENIALITY, 2000

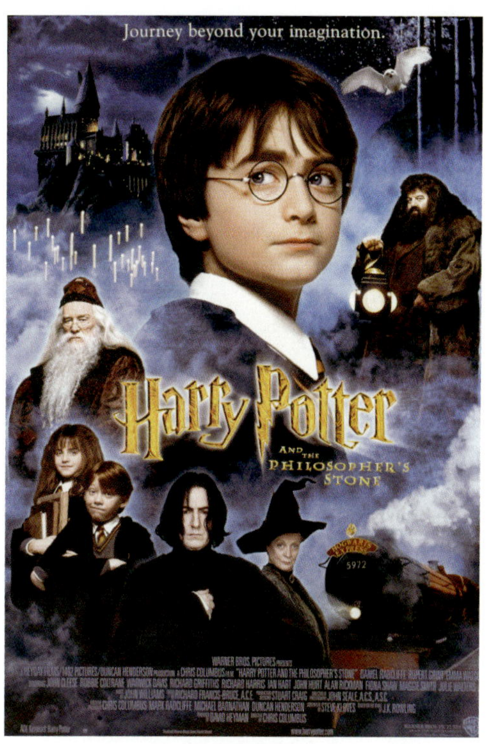

559. HARRY POTTER AND THE SORCERER'S STONE, 2001

560. TRAINING DAY, 2001

561. OCEAN'S ELEVEN, 2001

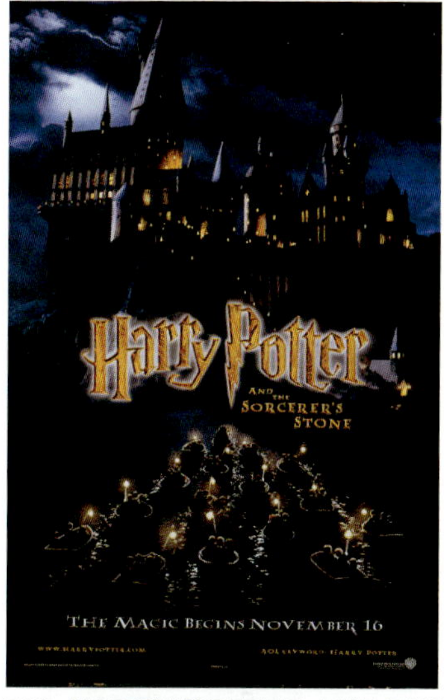

562. HARRY POTTER AND THE SORCERER'S STONE, 2001 (original English title)

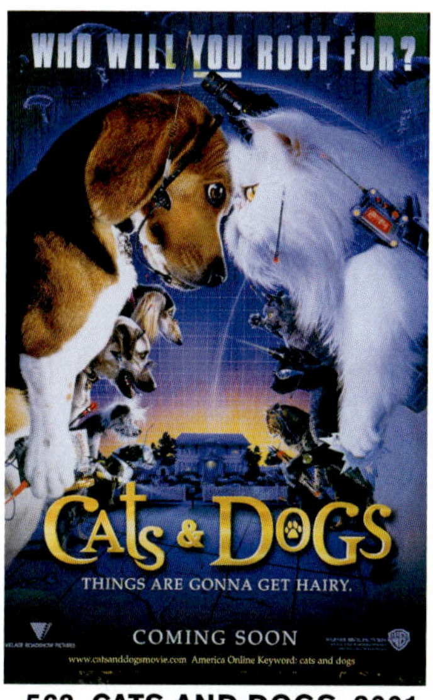

563. CATS AND DOGS, 2001

564. SWORDFISH, 2001

565. THE MAJESTIC, 2001

566. HARRY POTTER AND THE CHAMBER OF SECRETS, 2002

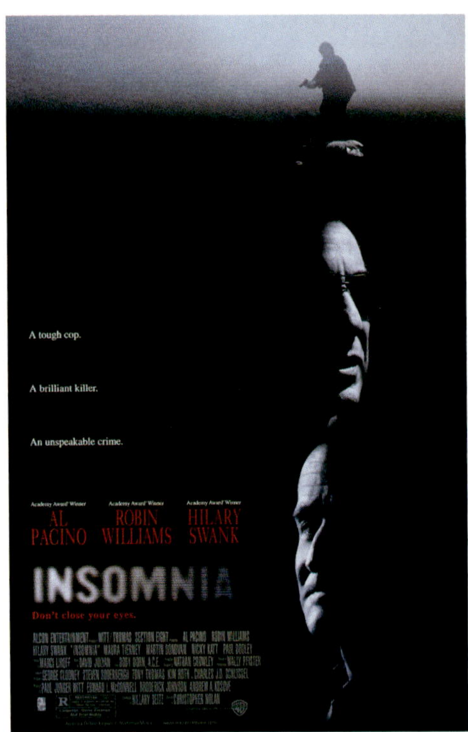

567. INSOMNIA, 2002

568. SCOOBY-DOO, 2002

569. THE MATRIX RELOADED, 2003

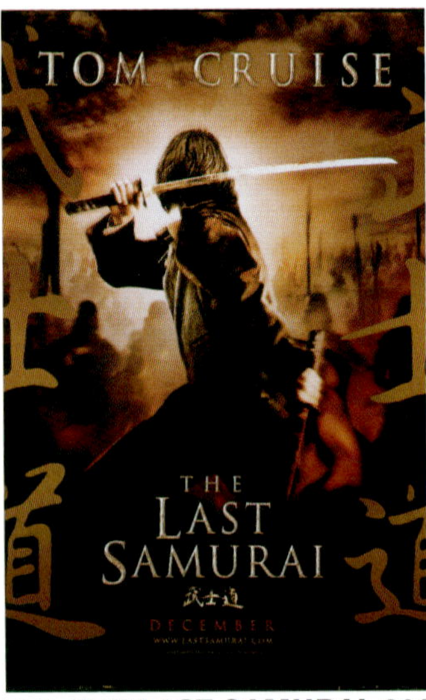

570. THE LAST SAMURAI, 2003

571. MYSTIC RIVER, 2003

572. A MIGHTY WIND, 2003

573. THE POLAR EXPRESS, 2004

574. TAKING LIVES, 2004

575. TROY, 2004

576. OCEAN'S 12, 2004

Warner Bros. Movie Posterl Index

Warner Bros. Movie Posterl Index